Japanese American Internment Camps

Other Books in the At Issue in History Series:

Japanese American Internment Camps

William Dudley, *Book Editor*

Daniel Leone, *President*
Bonnie Szumski, *Publisher*
Scott Barbour, *Managing Editor*

OPPOSING
VIEWPOINTS®
SERIES

AT ISSUE IN HISTORY

Greenhaven Press, Inc.
San Diego, California

Library of Congress Cataloging-in-Publication Data

Japanese American internment camps /
   William Dudley, book editor.
      p. cm. — (At issue in history)
   Includes bibliographical references and index.
   ISBN 0-7377-0820-4 (pbk. : alk. paper) —
ISBN 0-7377-0821-2 (lib. bdg. : alk. paper)
   1. Japanese Americans—Evacuation and relocation, 1942–1945. 2. World War, 1939–1945—Concentration camps—United States. 3. World War, 1939–1945—Japanese Americans.
I. Dudley, William, 1964– II. Series.

D769.8 A6 J3625 2002
940.53'17'0973—dc21

                                                            2001033804

Cover photo: © CORBIS
National Archives, 26, 108

© 2002 by Greenhaven Press, Inc., PO Box 289009,
San Diego, CA 92198-9009

Printed in the U.S.A.

Contents

Chapter 2: Constitutional Questions Raised by the Treatment of Japanese Americans

If this evidence questioning the military necessity of mass evacuation had not been suppressed, the Supreme Court may have ruled differently.

Chapter 3: Legacies and Lingering Disputes Concerning the Internment of Japanese Americans

Foreword

Historian Robert Weiss defines history simply as "a record and interpretation of past events." Both elements—record and interpretation—are necessary, Weiss argues.

Names, dates, places, and events are the essence of history. But historical writing is not a compendium of facts. It consists of facts placed in a sequence to tell a connected story. A work of history is not merely a story, however. It also must analyze what happened and *why*—that is, it must interpret the past for the reader.

For example, the events of December 7, 1941, that led President Franklin D. Roosevelt to call it "a date which will live in infamy" are fairly well known and straightforward. A force of Japanese planes and submarines launched a torpedo and bombing attack on American military targets in Pearl Harbor, Hawaii. The surprise assault sank five battleships, disabled or sank fourteen additional ships, and left almost twenty-four hundred American soldiers and sailors dead. On the following day, the United States formally entered World War II when Congress declared war on Japan.

These facts and consequences were almost immediately communicated to the American people who heard reports about Pearl Harbor and President Roosevelt's response on the radio. All realized that this was an important and pivotal event in American and world history. Yet the news from Pearl Harbor raised many unanswered questions. Why did Japan decide to launch such an offensive? Why were the attackers so successful in catching America by surprise? What did the attack reveal about the two nations, their people, and their leadership? What were its causes, and what were its effects? Political leaders, academic historians, and students look to learn the basic facts of historical events and to read the intepretations of these events by many different sources, both primary and secondary, in order to develop a more complete picture of the event in a historical context.

In the case of Pearl Harbor, several important questions surrounding the event remain in dispute, most notably the role of President Roosevelt. Some historians have blamed his policies for deliberately provoking Japan to attack in order to propel America into World War II; a few have gone so far as to accuse him of knowing of the impending attack but not informing others. Other historians, examining the same event, have exonerated the president of such charges, arguing that the historical evidence does not support such a theory.

The Greenhaven At Issue in History series recognizes that many important historical events have been interpreted differently and in some cases remain shrouded in controversy. Each volume features a collection of articles that focus on a topic that has sparked controversy among eyewitnesses, contemporary observers, and historians. An introductory essay sets the stage for each topic by presenting background and context. Several chapters then examine different facets of the subject at hand with readings chosen for their diversity of opinion. Each selection is preceded by a summary of the author's main points and conclusions. A bibliography is included for those students interested in pursuing further research. An annotated table of contents and thorough index help readers to quickly locate material of interest. Taken together, the contents of each of the volumes in the Greenhaven At Issue in History series will help students become more discriminating and thoughtful readers of history.

Introduction

World War II touched the lives of almost every American in the years from 1941 to 1945. However, one group was affected by the war in a unique fashion. During this time, approximately 110,000 U.S. citizens and resident aliens of Japanese ancestry were forced by the federal government to abandon their homes and possessions on the West Coast and move to remote government-constructed encampments, where they lived under armed guard. The wartime relocation and internment of most Japanese Americans residing in the continental United States is now a controversial, and for many, an ignoble chapter of American history. Historian James J. Martin has characterized it "as a breach of the Bill of Rights on a scale so large as to beggar the sum total of all such violations from the beginnings of the United States down to that time." Historians and legal scholars continue to debate its ramifications.

Much of the debate over Japanese-American internment has focused on the question of *why* the American government decided on (and most American people supported) this course of action. What were the reasons for Japanese removal, and were they, in hindsight, justified? Other studies have focused on the related question of how the Japanese Americans directly affected by internment reacted and whether (again in hindsight) accommodation or resistance to internment was the right response.

Military necessity—the idea that America needed to protect itself from possible treason and sabotage from its Japanese minority—was the official reason given by military commanders and War Department officials for excluding Japanese Americans from the West Coast and ultimately confining them to guarded centers. It was the reason given by state and local politicians in calling for Japanese exclusion, the reason for President Franklin Roosevelt's executive order authorizing the program, and the reason cited by the Supreme Court in upholding various relocation policies as constitutional in several landmark cases. This explanation was readily accepted by some internees themselves who actively cooperated with American authorities in their own internment as a way of proving their loyalty to America and assisting its war effort. More than forty years later, assistant war secretary John J. McCloy continued to defend the internment on these grounds:

> The President's action in ordering the relocation of Japanese/Americans from the sensitive military areas of the West Coast was entirely just and reasonable. . . . It was a calculated attempt on his part to offset the great menace to our security caused by the sinking of our main Pacific Fleet. The President had ample . . . evidence of the existence of subversive Japanese and Japanese/American agencies on the West Coast, poised to frustrate any defense against Japanese acts of aggression.

Others, however, have raised questions about whether the *official* reason was in fact the *real* reason for Japanese-American internment. Many historians now believe that the mass evacuation and internment did not meet a legitimate national security need, but was instead motivated by other factors, including racial prejudice and economic envy of the Japanese-American minority. Some internees also believed this at the time; some committed acts of resistance throughout their internment. In the early 1980s, an official group appointed by President Jimmy Carter, the Commission on Wartime Relocation and Internment of Civilians, concluded that internment was "not justified by military necessity" and was instead based on "race prejudice, war hysteria, and a failure of political leadership."

The internment remains a landmark and controversial event in American history, especially for those directly effected. "Whatever significance the relocation, as it is usually called, might have for American history in general," writes historian Roger Daniels, "it remains *the* central event of Japanese-American history." To provide some context for the articles in this volume, what follows is a brief overview of the Japanese-American community in 1941 and the various decisions that were made by and about them in subsequent years.

Japanese Americans in 1941

In 1941, the Japanese-American community in the continental United States consisted of approximately 125,000 people, most of whom resided in California, Washington, and Oregon (an additional 150,000 lived in Hawaii, then a U.S. territory). Many West Coast Japanese had attained a measure of economic success in farming and other pursuits. Most resided in segregated enclaves within cities or rural areas. The community's evolution was significantly affected by American immigration and naturalization law, which treated them differently from their counterpart immigrants from Europe.

Japanese Americans consisted of the "Issei" —first generation immigrants from Japan—and the "Nisei"—their American-born children. The Issei—the majority of whom were over the age of 50 by 1941—were the result of Japanese emigration to the United States. This migration began in the 1890s and ended with the Asian Exclusion Act of 1924, which barred Japanese immigration. Despite the passage of that federal law, the population of Japanese Americans continued to grow as those already in the United States had children. The Japanese-American population increased from 111,010 in 1920 to 126,947 in 1940, two-thirds of whom were Nisei.

Japanese immigrants, unlike those from Europe, could not choose to become naturalized U.S. citizens because federal law limited citizenship to "free white persons" and (after 1870) to "persons of African descent." Like Chinese immigrants and other Asians, the Issei held the legal status of "aliens ineligible for citizenship." As such, they were often the targets of discriminatory state laws, such as those in California banning land ownership to all "aliens ineligible for citizenship." Their Nisei children, on the other hand, were American citizens by virtue of their birth in the United States.

In 1941 three-quarters of the Nisei were under twenty-five years of age. In addition to differences in age and legal status, Nisei attitudes toward Japan and the United States were also often different from those of their parents. "While the Issei still identified with Japan to a certain extent," writes historian Leslie T. Hatamaya, "many of the Nisei ... were almost entirely America-oriented." The result was a "transformation from a predominantly Japanese-speaking immigrant group to an established ethnic community consisting primarily of English-speaking, American-born, American-educated citizens." (An exception merited its own Japanese term: The "Kibei" were children of Japanese-American immigrants born in the United States but sent to Japan for schooling.)

Circumstances changed dramatically for all Japanese Americans, both Issei and Nisei, following Japan's attack on Pearl Harbor on December 7, 1941. The surprise air attack cost the United States eight battleships, two hundred airplanes, and almost twenty-five hundred American lives. It also resulted in the entry of the United States into World War II against Japan and, soon after, Germany and Italy. Many Americans were searching for answers to the question of why Japan was so successful at Pearl Harbor—a search that for some led to broad accusations of Japanese-American espionage and sabotage.

The Pearl Harbor attack set forth a train of events that culminated in the internment of most Japanese Americans. This policy of relocation and internment took place in several distinct phases. Immediately after the attack, federal agents of the Department of Justice (DOJ) and Federal Bureau of Investigation (FBI) quietly rounded up suspicious "enemy aliens" in Hawaii and the United States. These included German and Italian as well as Japanese aliens, many of whom had been under monitoring by the FBI and other law enforcement authorities prior to the attack. By the end of 1941, two thousand Issei in Hawaii and the West Coast were arrested and taken to DOJ internment camps. Those arrested included community leaders such as newspaper editors, religious ministers and priests, and Japanese language teachers. Some were questioned and sent back home in a few weeks. Others were detained for several years in DOJ internment camps in Crystal City, Texas, and other locations.

These actions against individual Japanese leaders were not enough for some in California and other states. Newspaper columnist Henry McLemore called "for immediate removal of every Japanese on the West Coast to a point deep in the interior," a position echoed by political leaders including California governor Culbert Olson and organizations such as the Los Angeles Chamber of Commerce. Public clamor against Japanese Americans greatly increased at the end of January 1942, when an official government investigation of the Pearl Harbor attack chaired by Supreme Court Justice Owen Roberts alleged that Japanese Americans in Hawaii had spied for and otherwise abetted the Japanese attackers. News of Japan's sweeping early military successes in World War II increased public fears of attacks and even invasion by Japan as well as fears of spying and sabotage by agents within the United States. John L. De-Witt, chief of the army's Western Defense Command, was preoccupied with the possibility of another Pearl Harbor on his watch; in February he sent a memo to Secretary of War Henry Stimson recommending the removal of all citizens and aliens of Japanese ancestry from the West Coast. "The Japanese race is an enemy race," he wrote, adding that the "very fact that no sabotage has taken place to date" was a "disturbing and confirming indication that such action will be taken."

A President's Decision

On February 19, 1942, President Franklin D. Roosevelt issued Executive Order 9066. The order directed the War Department to "prescribe military areas . . . from which any and all persons may be excluded." The order did not specify Japanese Americans, but they were ultimately the only ones targeted as a group. Historian David M. Kennedy writes, "No explicit reference to the Japanese was necessary." The effect of Roosevelt's order was to place the fate of West Coast Japanese Americans in the immediate control of the U.S. military, specifically General DeWitt.

Following Roosevelt's order came a brief period of "voluntary withdrawal." DeWitt issued an order declaring the western halves of Washington, Oregon, and California and the southern half of Arizona as Military Area Number One. Japanese Americans were encouraged to voluntarily resettle outside that zone. Several thousand Japanese left the prohibited coastal zone on their own accord to live with relatives or friends in other parts of the country. Roosevelt created the War Relocation Authority (WRA), a civilian bureaucracy, to facilitate such voluntary resettlement. However, the prospect of eastward Japanese movement ran into opposition from neighboring states. The attorney general of Idaho, for example, contended that "all Japanese should be put in concentration camps" because "we want to keep this a white man's country." Other state governors and leaders—and in some cases armed posses and vigilantes—expressed similar sentiments about "Japs" coming into their midst.

Assembly Centers and Relocation Centers

On March 27, 1942, DeWitt issued a "freeze" order that prohibited Japanese Americans from moving from the Pacific Coast military zone without permission. In early April military orders were posted ordering all remaining citizens and aliens of Japanese descent in Military Area One and Military Area Two (the eastern half of California) to report to designated departure points. Instructed to bring along only what they could carry, many families were forced to sell or dispose of farms, businesses, and other property at depressed prices. The U.S. army then gave them numbered identification tags and transported them by bus or train to "assembly centers." These were hastily constructed barracks and facilities located in such places as horse racing tracks and state fair sites, where families were housed in converted horse stalls among other places. Within the next several months, they were moved once again to one of ten "relocation centers" that had been constructed in Arkansas, Arizona, Idaho, Wyoming, Colorado, Utah, and California. These centers, built and administered by the WRA and situated in remote areas, were to become their homes for the next few years.

Accommodations in the WRA camps consisted of spartan, military-style barracks. Families were housed in rooms furnished with cots and pot-bellied stoves and little else; internees used common latrines and ate in communal mess halls. The WRA directed camps to be self-sufficient in labor, but paid internees lower wages than were paid U.S. army privates. This meant that all Japanese internees, including professionals such as doctors and educators, made a fraction of what WRA personnel and other outside employees of the camps were paid.

With time and effort, the evacuees were able to transform and improve their living conditions. Gardens were created and cultivated; furniture was constructed out of scrap lumber. Schools, churches, libraries, newspapers, sports leagues, Boy Scout troops, and other community and social institutions were resurrected. The camps became,

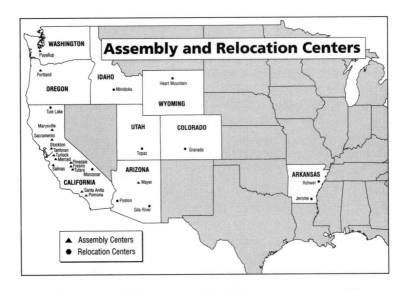

save for armed sentries and barbed wire fences, similar in some ways to other American small towns.

Camp life, as administered by the War Relocation Administration, exacerbated divisions within the Japanese-American community, especially between Nisei and Issei. The WRA gave great deference and leeway to one particular organization, the Japanese American Citizens League (JACL), a Nisei organization founded in 1930 that by 1941 had about seven thousand members. JACL leaders made the choice to cooperate with internment; they in turn were given prominence and authority by WRA administrators in managing the camps. Taking their advice, camp administrators limited community government to citizens, banned Japanese language schools, and prohibited the Japanese language at camp meetings. The actions effectively nullified whatever remaining authority traditional Issei leaders had within the community; some derided JACL members as "inu," or dogs. In some cases, tensions between camp factions erupted in violence.

Resettlement, Loyalty, and Segregation

Many WRA administrators viewed the relocation centers as a temporary fix to the problem of excluding Japanese Americans from the West Coast, and sought to reward "loyal" Japanese Americans with releases from the camps. As early as October 1942, Japanese Americans who were able to satisfactorily prove their loyalty to the WRA officials were permitted to leave for work furloughs or more permanent resettlement. Several thousand Nisei were permitted to enroll in colleges outside the exclusion zone. Others who found guaranteed housing and employment (often by religious or civic groups) were permitted to resettle outside the camps (but not return to the West Coast). In 1943 alone an estimated seventeen thousand evacuees were allowed to leave the camps and reenter civilian life. Most of them were Nisei between the ages of 18 and 30. When President Roosevelt in January 1943 approved the formation of a segregated Japanese-American regiment, military service became another alternative to the camps. Many young Nisei volunteered, thinking this a good chance to demonstrate their loyalty to the United States. Their choice was not always approved by their embittered parents. The 442nd Regiment, consisting of Japanese Americans from the camps and from Hawaii, fought in Europe and became one of the most decorated units in U.S. Army history.

In an attempt to increase military registration and resettlement outside the camps, the WRA in early 1943 made its "leave clearance form" mandatory for all camp residents seventeen and older. The form, which residents referred to as a "loyalty questionnaire," contained two questions in particular that caused much controversy and divided camps into "yes-yes" and "no-no" contingents. Question 27 asked: "Are you willing to serve in the armed forces of the United States on combat duty, wherever ordered?" Question 28 read

> Will you swear unqualified allegiance to the United States of America and faithfully defend the United States from any or all attack by foreign or domestic forces, and forswear any form of allegiance to the Japanese emperor, or any other foreign government, power, or organization?

Many internees found these questions troubling. Answering "no" to the questions would leave them open to charges of disloyalty and might result in their eventual deportation to Japan. Most internees eventually answered "yes" to both questions, but several thousand answered "no" to one or both questions or qualified their "yes" answers and were classified as "disloyal."

Reasons for answering "no" varied. Some felt the wording of Question 28 meant that a "yes" answer implied a *previous* allegiance to Japan. Issei, barred by federal law from attaining U.S. citizenship, were afraid that answering "yes" to the questions would leave them stateless. Some internees wanted to condition their loyalty on promises to improve conditions at the camps or to close them.

Eventually about eighty-five hundred internees of the "no-no" group were sent to the camp at Tule Lake, California, in an effort to segregate "troublemakers" from the rest of the internees. The segregation plan raised more legal questions about the mass evacuation scheme, which was based on the idea that all Japanese Americans were suspect. Yamato Ichihashi was a sixty-four-year-old Issei and a history professor at Stanford University who wrote an extensive diary of his experiences in the camps. In a letter to a Stanford colleague, he asked that if the government decided it could determine which Japanese Americans were loyal and which should be segregated as disloyal, "how could the American government continue to justify the present policy of keeping the loyal citizens and aliens in the relocation centers? It conflicts with the fundamental reason given for the wholesale evacuation."

Legal Challenges and Supreme Court Cases

Japanese-American evacuation and internment did receive several legal challenges during World War II, several of which reached the Supreme Court. In all of these cases the Court found Executive Order 9066 and military orders made under its authority to be constitutional. In *Hirabayashi v. United States* (1943), the Supreme Court upheld the conviction of Gordon Hirabayashi for violating a military curfew, approving of "differentiating citizens of Japanese ancestry from other groups in the United States." In *Korematsu v. United States* (1944), the Court upheld mass evacuation orders directed at Japanese Americans. In both cases, the justices declined to rule directly on the constitutionality of the internment camps themselves. The third case, *Ex Parte Endo*, decided at the same time as *Korematsu*, was a partial victory for Mitsuye Endo, a Japanese-American citizen who had filed a civil suit calling for her release from a camp and challenging the government's right to imprison a citizen without due process. Thirty months after she filed her challenge, the Court granted Endo her release and ruled that the WRA had exceeded its statutory authority in detaining any Japanese American whose disloyalty to the United States could not be proven. But the ruling did not expressly deal with the broader constitutional issues raised by Executive Order 9066 or other matters relating to evacuation and internment.

The Supreme Court's ruling in the *Endo* case was announced on December 18, 1944. On that same day, the WRA announced that all its centers were to be emptied within a year's time. The day before, on December 17, the military exclusion zone barring Japanese Americans from the West Coast was finally lifted by the new acting commander of the Western Defense Command, Major General Henry C. Pratt. Japanese Americans were free to return to the military exclusion zones as of January 2, 1945. Some elderly internees, fearful of prejudice and violent reaction outside the camps, and in some cases without any home to return to, were reluctant to leave. However, the WRA gave such internees $25 and transportation by train to their pre-war hometown. The Tule Lake Relocation Center was the last to close its doors, on March 20, 1946.

After the War

In the years since World War II those interned attempted to rebuild their lives. They received some compensation for tangible evacuation-related losses and damages in the 1948 Japanese American Evacuation Claims Act. About $28 million was paid to claimants, although estimates for damages were generally much higher (the Federal Reserve Bank of San Francisco estimated wartime property losses of Japanese Americans to reach $400 million). Far more meaningful to many Japanese Americans was the Walter-McCarran Immigration and Naturalization Act of 1952, through which the Issei were finally allowed to become naturalized citizens.

Many camp survivors were reluctant to discuss their experiences. Some later compared their emotional response of shame and anger to those experienced by rape victims. However, as years went by, former internees who were children in the camps and third-generation Japanese Americans (the "Sansei") began to ask more questions about the camps. In the late 1960s and early 1970s, some activists went on pilgrimages to internment sites, organized academic conferences, and sought to lobby the federal government for apologies and reparations. Their arguments gained credence with President Gerald Ford's presidential proclamation in 1976 formally repealing Executive Order 9066. Another significant turning point in the redress campaign was the creation in 1980 of a government commission to investigate Japanese-American internment. The Commission on Wartime Relocation and Internment of Civilians not only reviewed numerous government documents, but also solicited testimonies of camp survivors—a process that often encouraged survivors who had declined to discuss or dwell on past memories the opportunity to come to terms with their past. In 1988, acting on the commission's recommendations, Congress passed legislation giving $20,000 as partial restitution for every individual camp survivor.

The restitution payments may be viewed as a closing chapter to the story of Japanese-American internment, but that story continues to provoke interest, study, reflection, and controversy among Americans. *Japanese American Internment Camps: At Issue in History* provides a variety of perspectives from both primary sources and historical studies on the decision by President Roosevelt and others to relocate this particular group of people. It includes articles on the Supreme Court decisions regarding internment and their broader implications for civil liberties for all Americans. The volume also examines some of the ways this episode in American history continues to affect the United States and the Japanese-American community, including how disagreements between advocates of accommodation and resistance continue to divide that community. The articles selected present a small sampling of diverse views on Japanese-American internment, an event that continues to reverberate in contemporary American life.

Chapter 1

The Decision to Relocate West Coast Japanese Americans

1

Japanese Americans Pose a Serious Threat to National Security

Earl Warren

In the weeks and months following Japan's attack on Pearl Harbor on December 7, 1941, numerous political leaders and press commentators in California and other western states clamored for the removal of Japanese Americans, arguing that they posed a "fifth column" threat of organized sabotage. Among the most prominent of those arguing for removal was California attorney general Earl Warren. The following selection is taken from Warren's testimony before the Tolan Committee, a congressional committee investigating enemy alien activities. The attorney general (and future Supreme Court justice) argues that California is highly vulnerable to attack and sabotage and that American-born Japanese may be more dangerous than their immigrant parents. Warren's testimony occurred shortly after President Franklin D. Roosevelt issued Executive Order 9066 authorizing the U.S. military to exclude suspected enemies from sensitive areas, but before that order had been translated into the forced removal of Japanese Americans from the West Coast.

For some time I have been of the opinion that the solution of our alien enemy problem with all its ramifications, which include the descendants of aliens, is not only a Federal problem but is a military problem. We believe that all of the decisions in that regard must be made by the military command that is charged with the security of this area.

From Earl Warren's testimony before the House Select Committee Investigating National Defense Migration, Hearings on H.R. 113, 77th Cong., 2nd sess., February 21 and 23, 1942, pp. 11,010–18.

I am convinced that the fifth column activities of our enemy call for the participation of people who are in fact American citizens, and that if we are to deal realistically with the problem we must realize that we will be obliged in time of stress to deal with subversive elements of our own citizenry.

If that be true, it creates almost an impossible situation for the civil authorities because the civil authorities cannot take protective measures against people of that character. We may suspect their loyalty. We may even have some evidence or, perhaps, substantial evidence of their disloyalty. But until we have the whole pattern of the enemy plan, until we are able to go into court and beyond the exclusion of a reasonable doubt establish the guilt of those elements among our American citizens, there is no way that civil government can cope with the situation.

On the other hand, we believe that in an area, such as in California, which has been designated as a combat zone, when things have happened such as have happened here on the coast, something should be done and done immediately. We believe that any delay in the adoption of the necessary protective measures is to invite disaster. It means that we, too, will have in California a Pearl Harbor incident.

I believe that up to the present and perhaps for a long time to come the greatest danger to continental United States is that from well organized sabotage and fifth column activity.

Opportunities for Sabotage

California presents, perhaps, the most likely objective in the Nation for such activities. There are many reasons why that is true. First, the size and number of our naval and military establishments in California would make it attractive to our enemies as a field of sabotage. Our geographical position with relation to our enemy and to the war in the Pacific is also a tremendous factor. The number and the diversification of our war industries is extremely vital. The fire hazards due to our climate, our forest areas, and the type of building construction make us very susceptible to fire sabotage. Then the tremendous number of aliens that we have resident here makes it almost an impossible problem from the standpoint of law enforcement.

A wave of organized sabotage in California accompanied by an actual air raid or even by a prolonged black-out could not only be more destructive to life and property but could result in retarding the entire war effort of this Nation far more than the treacherous bombing of Pearl Harbor.

I hesitate to think what the result would be of the destruction of any of our big airplane factories in this State. It will interest you to know that some of our airplane factories in this State are entirely surrounded by Japanese land ownership or occupancy. It is a situation that is fraught with the greatest danger and under no circumstances should it ever be permitted to exist. . . .

I believe that . . . the greatest danger to continental United States is that from well organized sabotage and fifth column activity.

In order to advise the committee more accurately on this subject I have asked the various district attorneys throughout the State to submit maps to me showing every Japanese ownership and occupancy in the State. Those maps tell a story, a story that is not very heartening to anyone who has the responsibility of protecting life and property either in time of peace or in war.

To assume that the enemy has not planned fifth column activities for us in a wave of sabotage is simply to live in a fool's paradise. These activities, whether you call them "fifth column activities" or "sabotage" or "war behind the lines upon civilians," or whatever you may call it, are just as much an integral part of Axis warfare as any of their military and naval operations. When I say that I refer to all of the Axis powers with which we are at war.

It has developed into a science and a technique that has been used most effectively against every nation with which the Axis powers are at war. It has been developed to a degree almost beyond the belief of our American citizens. That is one of the reasons it is so difficult for our people to become aroused and appreciate the danger of such activities. Those activities are now being used actively in the war in the Pacific, in every field of operations about which I have read. They have unquestionably, gentlemen, planned such activities for California. For us to believe to the contrary is just not realistic.

Following the attack on Pearl Harbor, many Americans expressed sentiments of distrust and resentment toward their Japanese-American neighbors.

Unfortunately, however, many of our people and some of our authorities and, I am afraid, many of our people in other parts of the country are of the opinion that because we have had no sabotage and no fifth column activities in this State since the beginning of the war, that means that none have been planned for us. But I take the view that that is the most ominous sign in our whole situation. It convinces me more than perhaps any other factor that the sabotage that we are to get, the fifth column activities that we are to get, are timed just like Pearl Harbor was timed and just like the invasion of France, and of Denmark, and of Norway, and all of those other countries.

Invisible Deadline for Sabotage

I believe that we are just being lulled into a false sense of security and that the only reason we haven't had disaster in California is because it has been timed for a different date, and that when that time comes if we don't do something about it it is going to mean disaster both to California and to our Nation. Our day of reckoning is bound to come in that regard. When, nobody knows, of course, but we are approaching an invisible deadline.

The Chairman [Rep. John H. Tolan]: On that point, when that came up in our committee hearings there was not a single case of sabotage reported on the Pacific coast, we heard the heads of the Navy and the Army, and they all tell us that the Pacific coast can be attacked. The sabotage would come coincident with that attack, would it not?

Attorney General Warren: Exactly.

The Chairman: They would be fools to tip their hands now, wouldn't they?

Attorney General Warren: Exactly. If there were sporadic sabotage at this time or if there had been for the last 2 months, the people of California or the Federal authorities would be on the alert to such an extent that they could not possibly have any real fifth column activities when the M-day comes. And I think that that should figure very largely in our conclusions on this subject.

Approaching an invisible deadline as we do, it seems to me that no time can be wasted in making the protective measures that are essential to the security of this State. And when I say "this State" I mean all of the coast, of course. I believe that Oregon and Washington are entitled to the same sort of consideration as the zone of danger as California. Perhaps our danger is intensified by the number of our industries and the number of our aliens, but it is much the same. . . .

American-Born Japanese

I want to say that the consensus of opinion among the law-enforcement officers of this State is that there is more potential danger among the group of Japanese who are born in this country than from the alien Japanese who were born in Japan. That might seem an anomaly to some people, but the fact is that, in the first place, there are twice as many of them. There are 33,000 aliens and there are 66,000 born in this country.

In the second place, most of the Japanese who were born in Japan are over 55 years of age. There has been practically no migration to this country since 1924. But in some instances the children of those people have been sent to Japan for their education, either in whole or in part, and while they are over there they are indoctrinated with the idea of Japanese imperialism. They receive their religious instruction which ties up their religion with their Emperor, and they come back here imbued with the ideas and the policies of Imperial Japan.

There is more potential danger among the group of Japanese who are born in this country than from the alien Japanese who were born in Japan.

While I do not cast a reflection on every Japanese who is born in this country—of course we will have loyal ones— I do say that the consensus of opinion is that taking the groups by and large there is more potential danger to this State from the group that is born here than from the group that is born in Japan.

Mr. Arnold [Rep. Laurence F. Arnold]: Let me ask you a question at this point.

Attorney General Warren: Yes, Congressman.

Mr. Arnold: Do you have any way of knowing whether any one of this group that you mention is loyal to this country or loyal to Japan?

Attorney General Warren: Congressman, there is no way that we can establish that fact. We believe that when we are dealing with the Caucasian race we have methods that will test the loyalty of them, and we believe that we can, in dealing with the Germans and the Italians, arrive at some fairly sound conclusions because of our knowledge of the way they live in the community and have lived for many years. But when we deal with the Japanese we are in an entirely different field and we cannot form any opinion that we believe to be sound. Their method of living, their language, make for this difficulty. Many of them who show you a birth certificate stating that they were born in this State, perhaps, or born in Honolulu, can hardly speak the English language because, although they were born here, when they were 4 or 5 years of age they were sent over to Japan to be educated and they stayed over there through their adolescent period at least, and then they came back here thoroughly Japanese. . . .

I had together about 10 days ago about 40 district attorneys and about 40 sheriffs in the State to discuss this alien problem. I asked all of them collectively at that time if in their experience any Japanese, whether California-born or Japan-born, had ever given them any information on subversive activities or any disloyalty to this country. The answer was unanimously that no such information had ever been given to them.

Now, that is almost unbelievable. You see, when we deal with the German aliens, when we deal with the Italian aliens, we have many informants who are most anxious to help the local authorities and the State and Federal authorities to solve this alien problem. They come in voluntarily and give us information. We get none from the other source. . . .

Concerns over Vigilantism

There is one thing that concerns us at the present time. As I say, we are very happy over the order of the President yesterday [Executive Order 9066]. We believe that is the thing that should be done, but that is only one-half of the problem, as we see it. It is one thing to take these people out of the area and it is another thing to do something with them after they get out. Even from the small areas that they have left up to the present time there are many, many Japanese who are now roaming around the State and roaming around the Western States in a condition that will unquestionably bring about race riots and prejudice and hysteria and excesses of all kind.

I hate to say it, but we have had some evidence of it in our State in just the last 2 or 3 days. People do not want these Japanese just loaded from one community to another, and as a practical matter it might be a very bad thing to do because we might just be transposing the danger from one place to another.

So it seems to me that the next thing the Government has to do is to find a way of handling these aliens who are removed from any vital zone.

In the county of Tulare at the present time and in the county of San Benito and in other counties there are large numbers of the Japanese moving in and sometimes the suggestion has come from the place that they leave, that they ought to go to this other community. But when they go there they find a hostile situation. We are very much afraid that it will cause trouble unless there is a very prompt solution of this problem.

My own belief concerning vigilantism is that the people do not engage in vigilante activities so long as they believe that their Government through its agencies is taking care of their most serious problem. But when they get the idea that their problems are not understood, when their Government is not doing for them the things that they believe should be done, they start taking the law into their own hands.

That is one reason why we are so happy that this committee is out here today because we believe that it will help us solve this problem quickly, which is just as important as to solve it permanently. . . .

Japanese Land Ownership

Now, gentlemen, I have some maps which show the character of the Japanese land ownership and possessory interests in California. I will submit them at the time I submit a formal statement on the subject. These maps show to the law-enforcement officers that it is more than just accident, that many of those ownerships are located where they are. We base that assumption not only upon the fact that they are located in certain places, but also on the time when the ownership was acquired.

It seems strange to us that airplane manufacturing plants should be entirely surrounded by Japanese land occupancies. It seems to us that it is more than circumstance that after certain Government air bases were established Japanese undertook farming operations in close proximity to them. You can hardly grow a jackrabbit in some of the places where they presume to be carrying on farming operations close to all Army bombing bases.

Many of our vital facilities, and most of our highways are just pocketed by Japanese ownerships that could be of untold danger to us in time of stress.

So we believe, gentlemen, that it would be wise for the military to take every protective measure that it believes is necessary to protect this State and this Nation against the possible activities of these people.

2

Mass Evacuation of Japanese Americans Is Not Justified

Galen M. Fisher

Not all West Coast residents supported mass evacuation and relocation of Japanese Americans during World War II. One of the leaders of opposition to such a policy was Galen M. Fisher, whose 1942 testimony before a special Congressional committee investigating "Problems of Evacuating Enemy Aliens and Others from Prohibited Military Zones" is excerpted here. Fisher expresses his support for measures to protect the United States from disloyal agents and for President Franklin D. Roosevelt's Executive Order 9066, giving military commanders the authority to designate and protect special military zones. However, he argues that the mass evacuation of all Japanese residents, both citizens and aliens, would not help achieve the nation's goals of winning the war and maintaining national security. He concludes that at most a few hundred Japanese may be disloyal, and they should be investigated and interned on an individual basis.

Fisher resided in Japan for twenty-one years while serving as secretary of the Young Man's Christian Association (YMCA). In 1942 he was a research associate in the political science department at the University of California at Berkeley and a prime organizer of the Committee for National Security and Fair Play, a San Francisco–based organization that worked to uphold the civil rights of Japanese Americans. He was active on behalf of Japanese Americans throughout the war and authored several published articles criticizing their internment.

From Galen M. Fisher's testimony before the House Select Committee Investigating National Defense Migration, Hearings on H.R. 113, 77th Cong., 2nd sess., February 21 and 23, 1942, p. 11,199.

I fully accept as our paramount aim: Win the war—maintain national security. Therefore, I approve any measures for control of either aliens or citizens that may be required to achieve these ends, in line with the President's proclamation of February 20.

But I am convinced that the sweeping evacuation of Japanese residents, whether aliens or citizens, would hinder, not help, the attainment of these ends. Removal of persons of any race or nationality should be confined to such as special investigation shows to be dangerous or decidedly suspicious. Identification cards, fingerprinting and photographs are all desirable.

Reasons for Opposing Mass Evacuation

1. The huge numbers involved make sweeping evacuation impracticable. . . . There are in California over 90,000 Japanese residents alone, not to mention the much larger numbers of Germans and Italians.

2. No definite plans have been made by any Government department for settling or supervising large numbers of evacuees. The most specific plan I have heard of is that proposed by several Japanese-American citizens, graduates in agriculture, for establishing farm cooperatives, but that would require huge Government loans to accommodate the 50,000 rural Japanese resident population, and would not care for the many city dwellers who are unsuited to agriculture.

3. Some two-thirds—over 60,000—of the Japanese in California are American citizens. Very few of them are dangerous, if we may judge by the fact that during December only 2 or 3 of them were detained by the Federal Bureau of Investigation, and I have not heard of many more being detained since them. Evidently, the few who are found to be dangerous can be interned, without disturbing the large majority.

4. Several thousand citizens of Japanese parentage are serving in our armed forces. Keeping their morale high is desirable for military efficiency; but to evacuate their families, or even their alien parents alone, would impair their morale and breed disaffection among the whole body of Japanese-American citizens.

5. Any organized and extensive fifth-column activity by residents of Japanese stock would presumably have to be led

by experienced alien Japanese. Most of the natural leaders have already been detained, and others can be, without evacuating the thousands of rank and file Japanese.

6. Harsh treatment of the Japanese residents will give the military rulers of Japan the finest sort of propaganda to support their claim to be "the protectors and deliverers of the colored races of Asia from the arrogant and race-biased white nations." The Nazis have already made much of our maltreatment of the Negro. If we violate in any degree the equal rights of our fellow citizens of Japanese stock, we mock our pretensions of fighting to defend democracy.

7. Since we are confident of winning the war, the Japanese are a possible menace to our national security only during the war. Upon the coming of peace, we shall presumably wish them to continue as heretofore to take their place in our general life. If, however, we isolate them and give them cause to resent unnecessary discriminations imposed during the war, then they will not fit smoothly into our national life, but will present another acute race problem.

Trustworthy Citizens

8. Our citizens of Japanese parentage are just as trustworthy now as they were a few weeks ago when Governor [Cuthbert] Olson and other publicists paid tribute to their loyalty and civic devotion. Has the set-back given to the Allied arms by the military machine of Japan made our political leaders in State, county, and municipality play the bully and turn against our Japanese citizens as scapegoats for the remote culprits, in Japan, whom our Japanese-American citizens have repeatedly denounced? Like many other Americans who have long known hundreds of Japanese, I would testify that among their most marked traits are loyalty and gratitude. I strongly believe that the Nisei citizens [second generation Japanese Americans] will, with few exceptions, be as loyal to the United States as any other group of citizens. The exceptions are likely to be found chiefly among the Kibei, or American-born Japanese who are sent to Japan for their schooling, especially those who go before they have finished grammar and high school here. The Kibei, however, are reliably estimated to number less than a quarter of the total of the Nisei.

9. In connection with the whole question of citizens of Japanese stock, I wish to testify to the great service to our

Nation already rendered by the Japanese-American Citizens' League. It is the only inclusive organization touching the Nisei and it can be of great value in maintaining their undivided loyalty to the United States.

I . . . hope that a panicky public will not try to stampede our military and judicial authorities into evacuating . . . tens of thousands of people.

---

10. Little evidence pointing to fifth-column activity seems yet to have been discovered by the Federal Bureau of Investigation or the naval and military intelligence, although they have been hunting hard to find it. A high military authority recently told me that he took no stock in the alarmist predictions that fifth-columnists in California were only waiting for the ides of March. I hope that our intelligence services will not relax for a moment their vigilance, but I also hope that a panicky public will not try to stampede our military and judicial authorities into evacuating thousands or tens of thousands of people, in order to avert a possible danger that can probably be averted by evacuating a few hundreds. In all the clamor about the Japanese residents, it may be that we are overlooking a greater menace in the form of the Nazi partisans in our midst. The Japanese spies and saboteurs can be much more easily spotted because of their color and physiognomy than can Nazi or Italian plotters.

3

A Military Commander Recommends Evacuation

John L. DeWitt

On December 11, 1941, Lieutenant General John L. De-Witt, a sixty-one-year-old career army officer, was appointed to head the Western Defense Command, a region that included California, Oregon, Washington, Arizona, Nevada, Montana, Idaho, and Utah. Both contemporaries and historians have contended he was preoccupied with preventing any more surprises like Pearl Harbor and obsessed with possible Japanese attacks and sabotage. DeWitt at first proposed that all male enemy aliens (Japanese, German, and Italian) ages fourteen and over be relocated to the country's interior, but disagreed with proposals by the Los Angeles Chamber of Commerce and others to intern Japanese-American citizens. However, by February 1942, as the following excerpts from his "Final Recommendation" to Secretary of War Henry L. Stimson indicate, DeWitt was convinced that all Japanese— aliens and citizens—should be removed from the West Coast. In his memorandum, dated February 14, 1942, DeWitt argues that all Japanese Americans should be treated as potential security risks and that defending the United States against attack requires their evacuation. On February 19, President Franklin D. Roosevelt signed Executive Order 9066 providing the legal basis for the subsequent military evacuation of Japanese Americans. The next day DeWitt was appointed by Stimson as the military commander responsible for executing Roosevelt's directive.

From "Final Recommendation of the Commanding General, Western Defense Command and Fourth Army, Submitted to the Secretary of War," by John L. De-Witt, February 14, 1942.

Memorandum for: The Secretary of War, Subject: Evacuation of Japanese and Other Subversive Persons from the Pacific Coast.

1. In presenting a recommendation for the evacuation of Japanese and other subversive persons from the Pacific Coast, the following facts have been considered:

A. Mission of the Western Defense Command and Fourth Army.

I. Defense of the Pacific Coast of the Western Defense Command, as extended, against attacks by sea, land, or air;

II. Local protection of establishments and communications vital to the National Defense for which adequate defense cannot be provided by local civilian authorities.

B. Brief Estimate of the Situation.

I. Any estimate of the situation indicates that the following are possible and probable enemy activities:

a. Naval attack on shipping in coastal waters; b. Naval attack on coastal cities and vital installations; c. Air raids on vital installations, particularly within two hundred miles of the coast; d. Sabotage of vital installations throughout the Western Defense Command.

Hostile Naval and air raids will be assisted by enemy agents signaling from the coastline and the vicinity thereof; and by supplying and otherwise assisting enemy vessels and by sabotage.

Sabotage (for example, of airplane factories), may be effected not only by destruction within plants and establishments, but by destroying power, light, water, sewer, and other utility and other facilities in the immediate vicinity thereof or at a distance. Serious damage or destruction in congested areas may readily be caused by incendiarism.

II. The area lying to the west of the Cascade and Sierra Nevada Mountains in Washington, Oregon, and California, is highly critical not only because the lines of communication and supply to the Pacific theater pass through it, but also because of the vital industrial production therein, particularly aircraft. In the war in which we are now engaged racial affinities are not severed by migration. The Japanese race is an enemy race and while many second and third generation Japanese born on United States soil, possessed of United States citizenship, have become "Americanized," the racial strains are undiluted. To conclude otherwise is to expect that children born of white parents on Japanese soil sever all racial affinity and become loyal Japanese subjects, ready to fight and, if necessary, to die for Japan in a war against the nation of their parents. That Japan is allied with Germany and Italy in this struggle is no ground for assuming that any Japanese, barred from assimilation by convention as he is, though born and raised in the United States, will not turn against this nation when the final test of loyalty comes. It, therefore, follows that along the vital Pacific Coast over 112,000 potential enemies, of Japanese extraction, are at large today. There are indications that these are organized and ready for concerted action at a favorable opportunity. The very fact that no sabotage has taken place to date is a disturbing and confirming indication that such action will be taken.

The Japanese race is an enemy race.

C. Disposition of the Japanese.

1. Washington. As the term is used herein, the word "Japanese" includes alien Japanese and American citizens of Japanese ancestry. In the State of Washington the Japanese population, aggregating over 14,500, is disposed largely in the area lying west of the Cascade Mountains and south of an east-west line passing through Bellingham, Washington, about seventy miles north of Seattle and some fifteen miles south of the Canadian border. The largest concentration of Japanese is in the area, the axis of which is along the line Seattle, Tacoma, Olympia, Willapa Bay, and the mouth of the Columbia River, with the heaviest concentration in the agricultural valleys between Seattle and Tacoma, viz., the Green River and the Puyallup Valleys. The Boeing Aircraft factory is in the Green River Valley. The lines of communication and supply including power and water which feed this vital industrial installation, radiate from this plant for many miles through areas heavily populated by Japanese. Large numbers of Japanese also operate vegetable markets along the Seattle and Tacoma waterfronts, in Bremerton, near the Bremerton Navy Yard, and inhabit islands in Puget Sound opposite vital naval ship building installations. Still others are engaged in fishing along the southwest Washington Pacific Coast and along the Columbia River. Many of these Japanese are within easy reach of the forests of Washington

State, the stockpiles of seasoning lumber and the many sawmills of southwest Washington. During the dry season these forests, mills, and stockpiles are easily fired. . . .

2. Oregon. There are approximately four-thousand Japanese in the State of Oregon, of which the substantial majority reside in the area in the vicinity of Portland along the south bank of the Columbia River, following the general line Bonneville, Oregon City, Astoria, Tillamook. Many of these are in the northern reaches of the Willamette Valley and are engaged in agricultural and fishing pursuits. Others operate vegetable markets in the Portland metropolitan area and still others reside along the northern Oregon seacoast. Their disposition is in intimate relationship with the northwest Oregon sawmills and lumber industry, near and around the vital electric power development at Bonneville and the pulp and paper installations at Camas (on the Washington State side of the Columbia River) and Oregon City, directly south of Portland. . . .

The very fact that no sabotage has taken place to date is a disturbing and confirming indication that such action will be taken.

---

3. California. The Japanese population in California aggregates approximately 93,500 people. Its disposition is so widespread and so well known that little would be gained by setting it forth in detail here. They live in great numbers along the coastal strip, in and around San Francisco and the Bay Area, the Salinas Valley, Los Angeles, and San Diego. Their truck farms are contiguous to the vital aircraft industry concentration in and around Los Angeles. They live in large numbers in and about San Francisco, now a vast staging area for the war in the Pacific, a point at which the nation's lines of communication and supply converge. Inland they are disposed in the Sacramento, San Joaquin, and Imperial Valleys. They are engaged in the production of approximately 38 percent of the vegetable produce of California. Many of them are engaged in the distribution of such produce in and along the waterfronts at San Francisco and Los Angeles. Of the 93,500 in California, about 20,000 reside inland in the mentioned valleys where they are largely

engaged in vegetable production cited above, and 54,600 reside along the coastal strip, that is to say, a strip of coastline varying from eight miles in the north to twenty miles in width in and around the San Francisco bay area, including San Francisco, in Los Angeles and its environs, and in San Diego.

Approximately 13,900 are dispersed throughout the remaining portion of the state. In Los Angeles City the disposition of vital aircraft industrial plants covers the entire city. Large numbers of Japanese live and operate markets and truck farms adjacent to or near these installations. . . .

Recommendations

I now recommend the following:

I. That the Secretary of War procure from the President direction and authority to designate military areas in the combat zone of the Western Theater of Operations (if necessary to include the entire combat zone), from which, in his discretion, he may exclude all Japanese, all alien enemies, and all other persons suspected for any reason by the administering military authorities of being actual or potential saboteurs, espionage agents, or fifth columnists. Such executive order should empower the Secretary of War to requisition the services of any and all other agencies of the Federal Government, with express direction to such agencies to respond to such requisition, and further empowering the Secretary of War to use any and all federal facilities and equipment, including Civilian Conservation Corps Camps, and to accept the use of State facilities for the purpose of providing shelter and equipment for evacuees. Such executive order to provide further for the administration of military areas for the purposes of this plan by appropriate military authorities acting with the requisitioned assistance of the other federal agencies and the cooperation of State and local agencies. The executive order should further provide that by reason of military necessity the right of all persons, whether citizens or aliens, to reside, enter, cross, or be within any military areas shall be subject to revocation and shall exist on a pass and permit basis at the discretion of the Secretary of War and implemented by the necessary legislation imposing penalties for violation.

II. That, pursuant to such executive order, there be designated as military areas all areas in Washington, Oregon, and California, recommended by me to date for designation by the Attorney General as Category "A" areas and such additional areas as it may be found necessary to designate hereafter.

III. That the Secretary of War provide for the exclusion from such military areas, in his discretion, of the following classes of persons, viz.:

a. Japanese aliens. b. Japanese-American citizens. c. Alien enemies other than Japanese aliens. d. Any and all other persons who are suspected for any reason by the administering military authorities to be actual or potential saboteurs, espionage agents, fifth columnists, or subversive persons.

IV. That the evacuation of classes (a), (b), and (c) from such military areas be initiated on a designated evacuation day and carried to completion as rapidly as practicable.

That prior to evacuation day all plans be completed for the establishment of initial concentration points, reception centers, registration, rationing, guarding, transportation to internment points, and the selection and establishment of internment facilities in the Sixth, Seventh, and Eighth Corps Areas.

That persons in class (a) and (c) above be evacuated and interned at such selected places of internment, under guard.

That persons in class (b) above, at the time of evacuation, be offered an opportunity to accept voluntary internment, under guard, at the place of internment above mentioned.

That persons in class (b) who decline to accept voluntary internment, be excluded from all military areas, and left to their own resources, or, in the alternative, be encouraged to accept resettlement outside of such military areas with such assistance as the State governments concerned or the Federal Security Agency may be by that time prepared to offer. . . .

The number of persons involved in the recommended evacuation will be approximately 133,000. (This total represents all enemy aliens and Japanese-American citizens in Category "A" areas recommended to date.)

4

Japanese Americans Should Cooperate with Evacuation Plans

San Francisco News

On March 2, 1942, General John L. DeWitt, the military commander of the western region of the United States, issued Public Proclamation No. 1. The order designated portions of Washington, Oregon, California, and Arizona to be special military areas from which certain classes of people may be excluded; these classes included German, Italian, and Japanese enemy aliens as well as all persons of "Japanese ancestry." An accompanying press release indicated that all Japanese in these zones would eventually be evacuated. The anticipated withdrawal of Japanese Americans received much support from the press. In a March 6, 1942, editorial by the *San Francisco News*, reprinted here, Japanese Americans are urged to willingly cooperate with any evacuation plans that the U.S. military may devise. Such cooperation would demonstrate the loyalty of Japanese Americans to the United States and would also protect the Japanese from vigilante attacks, the editors of the newspaper conclude.

Japanese leaders in California who are counseling their people, both aliens and native-born, to cooperate with the Army in carrying out the evacuation plans are, in effect, offering the best possible way for all Japanese to demonstrate their loyalty to the United States.

From "The Best Way to Show Loyalty," editorial, *San Francisco News*, March 6, 1942.

Many aliens and practically all the native-born have been protesting their allegiance to this Government. Although their removal to inland districts outside the military zones may inconvenience them somewhat, even work serious hardships upon some, they must certainly recognize the necessity of clearing the coastal combat areas of all possible fifth columnists and saboteurs. Inasmuch as the presence of enemy agents cannot be detected readily when these areas are thronged by Japanese the only course left is to remove all persons of that race for the duration of the war.

Demonstrating Loyalty

That is a clear-cut policy easily understood. Its execution should be supported by all citizens of whatever racial background, but especially it presents an opportunity to the people of an enemy race to prove their spirit of cooperation and keep their relations with the rest of the population of this country on the firm ground of friendship.

Every indication has been given that the transfer will be made with the least possible hardship. General DeWitt's order was issued in such a way as to give those who can make private moving arrangements plenty of time to do so. All others will not be moved until arrangements can be made for places for them to go. They may have to be housed in temporary quarters until permanent ones can be provided for them, but during the summer months that does not mean they will be unduly uncomfortable.

Real danger would exist for all Japanese if they remained in the combat area.

Their property will be carefully protected by the Federal Government, their food and shelter will be provided to the extent they are not able to provide it for themselves, and they will be furnished plenty of entertainment and recreation. That is not according to the pattern of the European concentration camp by any means.

Danger for All Japanese

Real danger would exist for all Japanese if they remained in the combat area. The least act of sabotage might provoke angry reprisals that easily could balloon into bloody race riots.

We must avoid any chance of that sort of thing. The most sensible, the most humane way to insure against it is to move the Japanese out of harm's way and make it as easy as possible for them to go and to remain away until the war is over.

5

The Role of Racial Prejudice in Japanese-American Relocation

Geoffrey S. Smith

The official reason given for the relocation and eventual internment of Japanese Americans during World War II was military security. However, many historians have since argued that racial prejudice many Americans held against "Japs" was the real reason behind public support for mass evacuation. Historian Geoffrey S. Smith examines how feelings about race, reaction to the Pearl Harbor attack, and President Franklin D. Roosevelt's efforts to rally the American public behind the war effort may all have been factors in the decision by America's political and military leaders to evacuate and eventually incarcerate 120,000 American residents based on their ethnicity. Smith is a professor of history at Queen's University in Kingston, Ontario, Canada.

On October 20, 1938, the Columbia Broadcasting System aired an adaptation of H.G. Wells's *War of the Worlds*. With its spare narrative, Orson Welles's production of a fictional invasion of New Jersey by hostile Martians proved for many listeners indistinguishable from a live broadcast of real events.

To the astonishment of everyone, hundreds of thousands of Americans accepted the scenario; indeed, no other broadcast in history had produced commensurate panic. The response to the *War of the Worlds* prompted observers to question the potential effect of radio on a gullible populace. A

Excerpted from "Racial Nativism and Origins of Japanese American Relocation," by Geoffrey S. Smith, in *Japanese Americans: From Relocation to Redress*, edited by Roger Daniels, et al. (Salt Lake City: University of Utah Press, 1986). Reprinted by permission of The University of Washington Press.

New York Times writer observed that a voice "as dramatic as that of Orson Welles is a powerful instrument; it must learn to handle 'news' without the slightest color of melodrama."

Behind such advice lay suspicion that propaganda might lull citizens into dangerous slumber, or lure them into unwise political action. European totalitarianism had kindled in America fears of misleading political sophistry and the threat of dictatorship in America. In this context Franklin D. Roosevelt's emphasis upon public relations, epitomized by his press conferences and fireside chats, raised the threat of manipulated opinion. With war in Europe a definite possibility by October 1938, supporters and adversaries of continental democracy—and the Roosevelt administration itself— showed concern with fifth-column groups and subversive ideas. Thus it was not surprising that the broadcast grated upon a populace anxious to remain aloof from global turmoil.

At first glance, the *War of the Worlds* may seem a bizarre way to introduce an analysis of the origins of the tragedy that befell 120,000 Japanese Americans. Yet judging from the fear, irrational arguments, and overreaction that characterized government decision makers and a large majority of citizens, especially on the West Coast, the comparison is suggestive.

The intense opposition of Americans to the Japanese was racially based.

Pearl Harbor resurrected the image of Pacific Coast Japanese as advance agents of the dreaded "Yellow Peril," and subjected them, ultimately, to the most broadly based and effective nativist crusade in American history. The decisions to evacuate and to incarcerate the Japanese Americans illuminate several key sources of a powerful nativism that made this ethnic minority a likely if not inevitable target. The intense opposition of Americans to the Japanese was racially based, but also contained themes of ethnic and cultural countersubversion that tied the anti-Japanese crusade to previous nativist episodes.

The Pearl Harbor Defeat

Scholars suggest the difficulty in isolating any one factor as the basis of the nativism that resulted in evacuation. Nonetheless, one must underline the significance of Pearl Harbor—the worst defeat ever inflicted upon this country. That event produced a mix of disbelief, outrage, and anxiety in the United States, emotions that grew in the ensuing weeks as Japan dealt Allied forces in the Western Pacific an unexpected series of military reversals. . . .

What Japanese policymakers termed defensive measures to stem western imperialism, many Americans—especially on the West Coast—saw as evidence of something they had suspected since the early 1900s. Americans faced in the "Japs" an enemy that was perceived as a different species, "whose skull pattern," as Roosevelt put it, "being less developed than that of the Caucasians, might be responsible for their aggressive behavior." The fact remained, however, that a colored nation had defeated the world's leading Anglo-Saxon powers.

A Fear of Invasion and Sabotage

In the shadow of Pearl Harbor the fear of an actual invasion by Japan became acute. This concern was voiced by Secretary of the Navy Frank Knox, who reviewed the damage and condemned Hawaiian Japanese "traitors" for "the most effective fifth-column work that's come out of this war except in Norway." Knox left the impression, born out by subsequent opinion polls, that the Issei and Nisei were, like their Hawaiian counterparts, a "treacherous," "sly," "cruel," and "warlike" people.

A week later the official committee of inquiry, led by Supreme Court Justice Owen J. Roberts, released its report. The board criticized naval laxity at Pearl Harbor but also fingered Japanese secret agents as facilitating the attack. This assertion had no basis, but it fanned American antagonism toward Japanese Americans. The Roberts Commission report also suggested that the FBI had been hindered prior to Pearl Harbor by adhering too closely to constitutional guarantees of civil liberties.

With the federal government priming Americans with tales of Japanese Hawaiian perfidy, it did not matter that Japanese Americans in California comprised a paltry 1.4 percent of that state's total population. Nor did it register that a secret government investigation before Pearl Harbor, headed by journalist C.B. Munson, discovered a "remarkable, even extraordinary degree of loyalty" among the Hawaiian and

West Coast Japanese. Nor, finally, did it merit consideration that the Pacific Coast Nisei, through the Japanese American Citizens League, strongly defended their loyalty to the United States.

What weighed most in shaping regional and national opinion during the two months before FDR signed Executive Order 9066 was the simple fact that the nation had been "pushed around by a slant-eyed people to whom [it felt] racially superior." [William Lydgate, *What America Thinks*, 1944.] Quickly, racial nativism burgeoned, spearheaded by regional patriotic organizations, agricultural and fishing interests, and by "commercial buzzards" eager to take over Japanese American enterprise. These groups, with a long history as agitators, were joined by several influential publishers, editors, and columnists, as well as by reformers, labor leaders, and politicians.

In Los Angeles radio commentator John B. Hughes warned that "ninety percent or more of American-born Japanese are primarily loyal to Japan." Obedient and poised to strike, the Japanese would "die joyously for the honor of Japan." Seeking support for evacuation, Hughes predicted that unless authorities formulated an adequate policy, Californians would invoke vigilante law, with its code of "shoot first and argue later." Hearst columnist Henry McLemore observed that the war marked the end of the melting pot. "I am for immediate removal of every Japanese on the West Coast to a point deep in the interior," he wrote. "Herd 'em up, pack 'em off and give 'em the inside room in the badlands. Let 'em be pinched, hurt, hungry, and dead against it. . . . Personally, I hate the Japanese. And that goes for all of them."

Most California newspapers deprived the imputed Asian fifth columnists of all humanity.

Calm prevailed immediately after Pearl Harbor, but by late January pandemonium enveloped the West Coast. Though J. Edgar Hoover opposed evacuation, feeling that the FBI already had identified "supposed" Japanese agents, the bureau exacerbated fears by publicizing such seized "contraband" as cameras, binoculars, hunting knives, and the dynamite used by farmers to clear their land of tree stumps. Soon, most California newspapers deprived the imputed Asian fifth columnists of all humanity, describing them as "yellow men," "mad dogs," "Nips," and "yellow vermin." A Native Daughter of the Golden West inquired, "Did God make the Jap as he did the snake, did you hear the hiss before the words left his mouth? Were his eyes made slanting and the hiss put between his lips to warn us to be on our guard?" A mortician announced his preference to "do business with a Jap than an American." Thousands of dust-bowl refugees, meanwhile, themselves hapless victims of circumstance scant years before, joined the clamor, finding in the "yellow bellies" a group that allowed them new social respectability.

Demands for Evacuation

Demands for evacuation soon began to flow into Washington from California's congressional delegation. In the process, any goodwill the Japanese Americans possessed soon dissipated. Governor Culbert Olson, a liberal, epitomized the movement of "friends" of the Japanese, from support to condemnation. Before Pearl Harbor he insisted that even if war came, the state's Japanese retain equal protection under the law—a basic constitutional guarantee. But on December 8 he proposed that the Japanese observe house arrest "to avoid riot and disturbance." A few weeks later, Olson approved the abrupt firing of hundreds of Nisei civil servants and also called for evacuation. . . .

For the duration of the war, federal and state authorities found not one act of espionage or sabotage within either the mainland or Hawaiian Japanese communities.

For the duration of the war, federal and state authorities found not one act of espionage or sabotage within either the mainland or Hawaiian Japanese communities. Nevertheless, California Attorney General Earl Warren emphasized this point to the Tolan Committee in late February, after evacuation had been determined. A contender for governor, Warren knew that an anti-Japanese policy would be popular, and

in his testimony he confirmed the interpretation that innocent circumstances should be considered ominous. He
warned of the danger to security posed by the propinquity
of Japanese American enclaves to dams, bridges, harbors,
power stations, airports, and aviation factories. He did not
mention that in most instances these residences preceded
those facilities; he seemed, in fact, to designate any place
where the Japanese settled as "strategic."

What counted most was the absence of sabotage in
coastal regions. "The fifth column activities that we are to
get," he claimed, "are timed just like Pearl Harbor was
timed and just like the invasion of France, and of Denmark,
and of Norway, and all of those other countries." Californians had been "lulled into a false sense of security," and "the
only reason we haven't had disaster in California is because
it has been timed for a different date." Evacuation was "absolutely constitutional." Warren concluded in wartime
"every citizen must give up some of his rights." Although
Warren was not a crucial figure in the decision to relocate
the Japanese, and much later recanted his statements, his attitude typified those of pragmatic liberals nationwide.

Other Sources of Nativism

Racist pressure groups and politicians on the Pacific Coast
were by no means alone in their outcry. In the South and
Southwest, conservative congressmen Martin Dies of Texas
and John Rankin of Mississippi and Senator Tom Stewart of
Tennessee demonstrated their own belief in white suprem-
acy. Rankin had earned the reputation of a negrophobe and
anti-Semite during the 1930s, and in mid-February he reiterated the "war-of-the-worlds" theme by observing: "Once
a Jap always a Jap. You cannot change him. You cannot make
a silk purse out of a sow's ear." World War II was "a race
war," he concluded. "The white man's civilization has come
into conflict with Japanese barbarism [and] one of them
must be destroyed." Using an argument that he turned
against alleged communists later in the decade, he observed
that the Japanese "are pagan in their philosophy, atheistic in
their beliefs, alien in their allegiance, and antagonistic to
everything for which we stand." Rankin's comments received strong backing from congressmen William F. Nor-
rell of Arkansas, Jennings Randolph of West Virginia, and
Schuyler O. Bland of Virginia.

Dies, the chairman of the House Un-American Activities Committee, had made an industry during the preceding four years of chasing fifth columns. A great self-promoter, he announced on January 28 that had his committee been allowed to reveal "facts" it possessed the previous September, "Pearl Harbor might have been averted." Unless Washington alerted itself to the problem, there would occur on the West Coast "a tragedy that will make Pearl Harbor sink into insignificance with it." On February 9, Dies lamented anew that Washington remained "lax, tolerant, and soft toward the Japanese who have violated American hospitality; Shinto Temples still operate; propaganda outlets still disseminate propaganda material; and Japanese, both alien and American citizens, still spy for the Japanese government."

One is tempted to dismiss such claptrap as a prime example of the paranoid style in American politics—the monopoly of fringe groups that exert little impact upon national policy. But, unfortunately, similar nativist sentiments infused the entire political spectrum, encompassing liberals like Warren, Mayor Fiorello La Guardia of New York, journalist Walter Lippmann, and Representative John Dingell of Michigan (who *before* Pearl Harbor suggested incarcerating 10,000 Hawaiian Japanese as hostages to ensure Tokyo's good behavior), and leftists like Vito Marcantonio and Carey McWilliams, and the editors of the Communist *Daily Worker* and *People's World*, each of whom found the fight against militarism and fascism more important than the civil liberties of Japanese Americans.

Hatred directed at the suspected (and powerless) Asian adversary within provided both a vicarious means of striking back at an unexpectedly awesome enemy and a source of unity and welcome consensus after the great foreign policy debate of 1941. . . .

The DeWitt Clique

Lieutenant General John L. DeWitt, head of the Western Defense Command, [was] entrusted by Roosevelt with the defense of the Pacific Coast. This elderly bureaucrat had more experience in supply than in combat and drew little respect from other army brass. He was cautious, indecisive, galled, no doubt, by seeing younger officers promoted throughout the army, and panic stricken lest he suffer a fate similar to his Hawaiian counterpart, Lieutenant General

Walter C. Short. Yet in the month after Pearl Harbor, De-Witt appeared content to leave the problem of enemy aliens to the Justice Department.

DeWitt initially approved "any preferential treatment to any alien irrespective of race," but his position shifted during the next six weeks. There were, to be sure, some scruples to overcome—for example, a policy emphasizing enemy ethnicity instead of race, per se, precluded action against Japanese aliens not also taken against German and Italian aliens. Yet the size of the latter groups, their political power, and their high degree of assimilation, made evacuation unthinkable. Moreover, action only against enemy aliens would prevent moving against the Nisei who were, after all, citizens. The Nisei were considered a greater threat than the Issei by some, but they could not be evacuated and their elderly parents left behind.

As late as February 3, Stimson observed that "we cannot discriminate among our citizens on the ground of racial origin." These views soon became casualties in the battle for control of the issue between the War and Justice departments. In this contest DeWitt became an important pawn, a spokesman for Major Karl R. Bendetsen, chief of the Aliens Division, Provost Marshal General's Office, and the latter's superior, Allen Gullion, who strongly desired not only removal of the Japanese from the West Coast but also sought to wrest control of enemy aliens from Attorney General Francis Biddle. Throughout the decision-making period, Gullion called the shots while Chief of Staff George C. Marshall "had little to do during January and February with the plans and decisions for Japanese evacuation."

The DeWitt clique became, in fact, the *diabolus ex machina* of relocation. "Military necessity" was the doctrine invoked—a transparent mantle, it soon became clear, for an elite nativism that ultimately breached the Bill of Rights [James J. Martin writes] "on a scale so large as to beggar the sum total of all such violations from the beginnings of the United States down to that time." By mid-February the professional soldiers and their civilian superiors—especially Stimson and his assistant, John J. McCloy—had reached conclusions about the Nisei "problem" that were indistinguishable from the warnings from western politicians and patriotic organizations. . . .

Bendetsen, who with Gullion exerted strong pressure

on McCloy and Stimson, felt certain that a Japanese invasion was possible and doubted that the Nisei "could with-
stand the ties of race and affinity" with the land of their fa-
thers. Stimson himself needed little prodding. Doubting the
capacities and patriotism of brown, yellow, and black Americans, he noted in his diary on February 10 that "an invisible deadline was approaching" and the "racial characteristics" of the Nisei predisposed them to potential disloyal
behavior.

Influenced by Bendetsen and Gullion, DeWitt reacted
similarly. "In the war in which we are now engaged," he
wrote Stimson on February 14, "racial affinities are not severed by migration. The Japanese race is an enemy race, and
while many second- and third-generation Japanese born on
United States soil, possessed of United States citizenship,
have become 'Americanized,' the racial strains are undiluted. . . . It therefore follows that along the vital Pacific
Coast over 112,000 potential enemies of Japanese extraction
are at large today." "A Jap's a Jap," he proclaimed later, "and
that's all there is to it."

---

*Through the War Department, anti-Japanese
racial nativism became national policy.*

Through the War Department, anti-Japanese racial nativism became national policy on February 19, when FDR
authorized the military to evacuate "dangerous persons"
from specified coastal areas and to erect inland concentration camps to hold them. Attorney General Biddle failed to
prevent the issue from passing to War Department control,
feeling—perhaps because he was new to the cabinet—un-
ready to oppose Stimson, "whose wisdom and integrity I
greatly respected." FDR, meanwhile, expressed satisfaction
that the question had reached Stimson's hands. . . .

Roosevelt and Race

In private moments Roosevelt himself exhibited some dubious views on race, including thoughts about crossbreeding
Europeans and Asians to extinguish Japanese delinquency.
On one occasion he told Treasury Secretary Henry Mor-
genthau that "you either have to castrate the German
people or you have to treat them in such a manner that they

can't just go on reproducing people who want to continue the way they have in the past." FDR also scorned the Burmese as "dislikeable," and he would inform Joseph Stalin at Yalta that the Vietnamese were "a people of small stature . . . and not warlike.". . .

In private moments Roosevelt himself exhibited some dubious views on race.

FDR was no political cousin of the Beast of Berchtesgaden, but his views underline D.W. Brogan's observation that "in the years between the wars, the United States was only outdistanced by Germany as a market for race theories, some of them crude enough to have suited Hitler." Thus Roosevelt's correspondence with Dr. Ales Hrdlicka, an idiosyncratic anthropologist at the Smithsonian, commands more than passing interest. Throughout the 1930s Hrdlicka warned him that Japan's leaders were "utterly egotistic, tricky, and ruthless" men, "working steadily towards the exclusion of all, and particularly the white man, from the Pacific and Eastern Asia.". . . Although not endorsing Hrdlicka's extremism, FDR did ask him in the early weeks of the war to undertake a study of race-crossing of Asian and European stocks. If the Japanese could be driven back to their islands, Roosevelt believed, perhaps their aggressive characteristics might be bred out of them.

If the connection between this assumption and Executive Order 9066 remains debatable, FDR's racial perspectives did make it easier for him to deprive Japanese Americans of their liberties. In fact, questions of race and civil liberties became interlocking expedients as the administration moved to cement national unity after Pearl Harbor. . . . With Pearl Harbor Roosevelt stepped up his demand that Hoover and Attorney General Biddle get rid of all traitors. Although Biddle hoped to avoid the "extravagant" civil liberties abuses of World War I, FDR peppered him and Hoover with ultimata about the disloyal. . . .

By discrediting perceptive noninterventionists, the administration identified its opponents as subversives. After Pearl Harbor Roosevelt told Churchill that a free press had become an additional burden, urged Biddle to get grand juries into action against his critics, and asked Hoover several times whether the director had cleared the Washington hotels of their "alien waiters."

A Quest for National Unity

The decision to relocate the Japanese Americans was consistent with the administration's prewar attitudes and policies toward objectionable minorities. Having proscribed the ideological marketplace, the federal government found it easy to shut down the ethnic marketplace for a group ill-equipped to defend itself. In fact, relocation was the tribute that administration pragmatism paid expediency. The quest for domestic unity early in 1942 had become both less and more of a problem: If isolationism lay buried with the fleet at Pearl Harbor, most Americans—two-thirds according to one poll—called upon the president to direct U.S. forces against Japan before counterattacking in Europe. Public opinion thus jeopardized Roosevelt's desire for a smoothly functioning Anglo-American alliance, as well as the conviction that European operations should precede any large-scale response in the Pacific.

While defending the Allied war effort as part of "the great upsurge of human liberty of the Bill of Rights and individual freedom against Nazi barbarism," the president did not take unity for granted. Roosevelt recognized the need to strike symbolic and substantive blows against Tokyo to counter what he construed as a mood of public demoralization. Toward these ends he ordered supplies flown to Chiang Kai-shek, made plans for sixteen B-25s to bomb Tokyo, and ordered General Douglas MacArthur to Australia to assume command of American forces in the Southwest Pacific.

And four days after the fall of Singapore, FDR signed Executive Order 9066, finding still another way "to relieve feelings of powerlessness towards Japan, and to quiet a potentially divisive issue." Recognizing that relocation centers were essentially concentration camps, Roosevelt realized the shaky constitutional ground he occupied and cautioned the army "to be as reasonable as you can." From the lack of opposition to the measure, Roosevelt knew that it would be popular, and, besides, 1942 was an election year. If relocation might help western Democrats in their quest for reelection, the move would strengthen bipartisanship since the cabinet's Republican appointees, Knox and Stimson, remained adamant for evacuation. . . .

In all these considerations, the quest for national unity remained paramount. If the army proved mistaken about the West Coast Japanese, FDR felt that was too bad; the military was fighting the war, and to oppose the military would be to court disunity and disaster.

The sundering of the constitutional rights of the Japanese minority had its origins in three centuries of American racial nativism. The episode might be compared to other forced relocations—those of American Indians during the nineteenth and twentieth centuries and of African blacks during the eighteenth and nineteenth. In the case of the Japanese, as with other minorities, legal status was defined by the dynamic of Caucasian hegemony interacting with expectant capitalism—with few countervailing forces to oppose Roosevelt's executive order and the forces that lay behind it.

The sundering of the constitutional rights of the Japanese minority had its origins in three centuries of American racial nativism.

Socialist leader Norman Thomas, American Civil Liberties Union attorney A.L. Wirin, and a few others demonstrated courage in opposing relocation, but the power at their command was merely moral, and their impact proved even less telling than the opposition against the earlier majorities mustered by the abolitionists, friends of the native Americans, or, for that matter, anti-imperialists at the turn of the century. California, apparently, remained the white "racial frontier" so celebrated since the days of the Gold Rush.

Knowing little or nothing of the diversities within Japanese American culture, nativists ascribed to this vulnerable, "middleman" minority a tightly knit organization that did not exist; a single-minded allegiance to a hostile power; a nonexistent incredible fecundity; an imaginary economic rapacity; and an unwillingness to become "Americanized," which existed because the Caucasian majority deemed that it should.

Perhaps, as Mayor Fletcher Bowron of Los Angeles conceded on February 6, 1942, the Japanese could not be trusted in the present emergency precisely because of the discrimination Californians had visited upon them. From the perspective of four decades, however, such an observation provides no consolation.

6

The Relocation of Japanese Americans Was Not a Racist or Shameful Episode

Dwight D. Murphey

Dwight D. Murphey is an attorney, a professor of business law at Wichita State University, and associate editor of *Conservative Review*. He has written extensively on social and political philosophy; his books include *Socialist Thought* (1983) and *Liberalism in Contemporary America* (1992).

Murphey contends that most American history writing and teaching is marred by what he calls a "deep animus against the United States" that he traces in part to leftist political activists and radicals of the 1960s. Former protesters, now college professors and community activists, have sought to demonstrate that the United States is a fundamentally unjust and racist society, he believes, and have seized on incidents such as the internment of Japanese Americans as evidence of such injustice. In the following essay, Murphey describes his findings from his own investigation into the World War II relocation of Japanese Americans. He questions whether "internment" is the proper word for what took place, arguing that many Japanese resettled outside the camps during the war. He also examines the military context in which the decision for mass relocation was made and contends that American political leaders had substantial reason to believe that the Japanese-American community posed a potentially serious threat to American security. Murphey downplays the role racial prejudice may have played in the

Excerpted from "The World War II Relocation of Japanese-Americans," by Dwight D. Murphey, *Journal of Social, Political, and Economic Studies*, Spring 1993. Reprinted by permission of the author.

decision for mass relocation and concludes that this episode of history, although regrettable, is not something for which Americans should feel shame.

━━━━━━━━━━━━━━━━━━━━━━━━━━━━━━━━━━

M any aspects of American life and history have come under attack by those who feel a deep alienation against the mainstream of American society. This hostile critique has been especially intense since the 1960s, but reflects a long-term phenomenon which has been one of the main facts about the United States since as long ago as the 1820s: the "alienation of the intellectual." The American people are not above criticism. It would be foolish to defend them categorically with regard to everything that has happened over their long history. And yet, I am persuaded that they are not and have not been, as a people, "befouled," as the critics from the Left have long wished us to believe.

Several issues have been most salient as part of the Left's attack. As to them, the existing literature is overwhelmingly one-sided, presenting a hostile critique. Is there "another side"?

In . . . essays that I wrote for the *Journal of Social, Political and Economic Studies* and the *Conservative Review* in the early 1990s, I approached each of these issues with a simple question: "What would a scholar, seeking to be thorough and objective, and yet at the same time not bringing to the subject a deep animus against the United States, think about what happened?". . .

The United States Did Not Act Shamefully

When I started my study of the removal of the Japanese-Americans I knew virtually nothing about it, and I have remained ready to report whatever I found. It obviously should not be a disqualification, though, for a scholar to begin his study of any of these issues without a prior animus against the United States.

Nor should proving the scholar's "objectivity" require him to find reason for America to be ashamed when that isn't called for. In my opinion, the United States did *not* act shamefully in its treatment of persons of Japanese ancestry during World War II. In fact, a better case could be made for a diametrically opposite criticism: that the treatment was so tender-hearted that it actually endangered the security of the United States during a desperate war.

In the intolerant context of today's ideological arguments, it is predictable that a conclusion favorable to the United States will be represented as "offensive" to the many splendid people of Japanese ancestry who now form a part of the American people. But that, of course, is nonsense. The search for historical accuracy isn't a panderer's game to curry favor. To seek the truth is no slander against anyone. . . .

In my opinion, the United States did not act shamefully in its treatment of persons of Japanese ancestry during World War II.

There is so much to the subject that it will be helpful for me to start, like a debater, by "telling you what I am going to tell you." Most of what follows will relate to two large questions:

• First, what exactly was done regarding the persons of Japanese ancestry?

• Second, why was it done?; i.e., what was its necessity? . . .

The First Question: What Was Done?

Immediate arrest of "dangerous aliens" after Pearl Harbor. Within days after the December 7, 1941, Japanese attack on Pearl Harbor, approximately 3,000 Japanese aliens classified as dangerous were arrested and incarcerated by the Department of Justice. These were individuals under suspicion by American intelligence agencies, which beginning in 1939 had begun to compile lists of persons considered dangerous in case of war. (This group was included among those who received an apology and $20,000 each in the early 1990s for "mental suffering.")

Declaration of the West Coast as a military zone; exclusion of persons of Japanese origin. On February 19, 1942, President Franklin D. Roosevelt signed Executive Order 9066. This authorized the establishment of military areas from which people of all kinds could be excluded. Lt. General John L. DeWitt was appointed the military commander to carry out the Executive Order. In March, Gen. DeWitt declared large parts of the Pacific Coast states military areas in which no one of Japanese descent would be allowed to remain. The exclusion order affected Japanese-Americans living on the West Coast by forcing them to move inland. Its only effect upon those who already lived inland was to bar them from going to the quarantined areas on the West Coast.

Col. Karl R. Bendetsen was named Director of the Wartime Civil Control Administration to handle the evacuation. Also in March, Roosevelt created a civilian agency, the War Relocation Authority (WRA), to assist the evacuees. Milton Eisenhower, brother of later president Dwight Eisenhower, was named Director. Congress ratified the evacuation by enacting legislation that made it a federal offense for anyone to violate the exclusion order.

A short-lived plan originally was to assist the Japanese-Americans in a process by which they would move inland "on their own recognizance" as individuals and families. Bendetsen [in 1981 testimony before the Commission on Wartime Relocation and Internment of Civilians] says that "funds were provided for them [and] we informed them . . . where there were safe motels in which they could stay overnight." This was ended almost immediately, by late March, however; Bendetsen says that the need for a more organized system became apparent when most of the Japanese-Americans were not able to make arrangements to relocate quickly even with some help. A second reason was that the governors of western states (reflecting public opinion in their states) objected strongly to thousands of people of Japanese origin moving into their states without oversight. These objections were reiterated at a Governors' Conference for ten western governors on April 7. (There was a continuing tension, lessening over time, between the desire to let the evacuees relocate freely and the public's desire to have them closely monitored.)

Assembly Centers

This led to the "assembly center phase," during which the evacuees were moved to improvised centers such as race tracks and fairgrounds along the West Coast pending the construction of ten "relocation centers" in eastern California, Arizona, Utah, Idaho, Wyoming, Colorado, and as far east as Arkansas. During this phase, federal officials made extensive efforts to lessen public hostility. As those feelings subsided, approximately 4,000 families moved inland "on their own recognizance" to communities of their choice before the assembly center phase was over at the end of the summer of 1942. Bendetsen says that all of the Japanese-Americans could have moved on their own at any time if they had seen their way clear to do it.

The government worked with the evacuees to take extraordinary measures to make the [assembly] centers as comfortable as possible.

The assembly centers are criticized as having had "barbed wire and searchlights," overcrowding, lack of privacy, and inadequate medical care. But Bendetsen disputes virtually all of this, as we will see in my later discussion of whether the evacuees can properly be said to have been "interned." Hastily improvised and purely temporary quarters for thousands of people who have been uprooted from their homes on short notice could not have been pleasant. There is no incongruity, however, between this and the fact, also true, that the government worked with the evacuees to take extraordinary measures to make the centers as comfortable as possible. In the short time they existed, some centers opened libraries; movies were shown regularly; there were Scout troops, arts and crafts classes, musical groups, and leagues for basketball and baseball. Three hundred and fifty people signed up for a calisthenics class at Stockton. All had playgrounds for children, and one even had a pitch-and-putt golf course. The centers were run almost entirely by the Japanese-Americans themselves.

As the ten relocation centers became ready, the evacuees were moved to them from the assembly centers. These were under the jurisdiction of the War Relocation Authority. Dillon S. Myer became the Director of the WRA in June when Milton Eisenhower resigned to become the deputy director of the Office of War Information. The relocation centers' highest population, of 106,770, was attained on November 1, 1942. The construction of the camps was of the type used for housing American soldiers overseas—which is to say, the centers were austere but functional. Senator S. I. Hayakawa later described them [in *Through the Communication Barrier*, 1979] as "dreary places: long rows of tarpaper-covered wooden barracks. . . . Each room had a stove, a drop light, an iron cot and mattress. . . . But the WRA," he said, "headed by the wise and humane Dillon Myer, . . . made life as comfortable as possible for them." It is worth noting that no families were ever separated during the process. . . .

Tule Lake Center used for actual internment. The center at Tule Lake, California, started as a relocation center but was soon turned into an actual internment camp—a "segregation center"—for those Japanese-Americans who were hostile to the United States. It housed those who applied to be repatriated to Japan if they had not withdrawn the application by the middle of 1943; those who answered "no" to a loyalty questionnaire and didn't clear up the problem in special hearings held for the purpose; those against whom the government had evidence of disloyalty; and the family members of those in the first three groups. . . .

Concentration Camps?

Were the relocation centers an "internment"? There is no question but that the evacuees were forced by law to leave their homes on the West Coast and to either stay in the centers or relocate elsewhere in the United States by receiving leaves for the purpose. Their exclusion from the West Coast was not voluntary, and after the short-lived initial phase their relocation had to be done through the centers, which granted leave, temporary or indefinite, for the purpose. But, except for those arrested as "dangerous aliens" right after Pearl Harbor and those who were later segregated at Tule Lake, were the Japanese-Americans "interned" in the centers? And were the centers, as is often charged, "concentration camps"?

It is important to realize that these questions are largely issues of characterization. Those who want to place the evacuation in the worst light stress the "humiliation" and "affront to our loyalty" inherent in being made to relocate. They especially like to speak of the centers as "concentration camps," thereby evoking images of the horrors of Nazi concentration camps. . . .

The substance of the charge of "internment" is contradicted by the fact that resettlement outside the centers was diligently pursued throughout the process. Hayakawa says that by January 2, 1945, half of those evacuated had "found new jobs and homes in mid-America and the East." What is most often pointed to in support of the charge of "internment" and even of the centers' being "concentration camps" is that there were "fences and guards." Even Hayakawa speaks of the centers as being "behind barbed wire, guarded by armed sentries." Oddly, however, the role of fences and guards depends largely upon perception.

In 1984 a House subcommittee asked Bendetsen about earlier testimony that there had been barbed wire and watchtowers, and he testified that "that is 100 percent false. . . . Because of the actions of outraged U.S. citizens, of which I do not approve, it was necessary in some of the assembly centers, particularly Santa Anita, . . . to protect the evacuees . . . and that is the only place where guards were used. [As to] relocation centers . . . there was not a guard at all at any of them. That would not be true of Tule Lake [after it became a segregation center]."...

Photographs are provided in some of the literature showing watchtowers and guards. As to each photograph, it is important to know the specific date and location. The persons at Tule Lake, for example, *were* under guard to keep them in; and photographs from early 1942 would relate to the assembly center phase.

As we will see in my discussion of the military situation, there were strong reasons for an actual internment, which is what Earl Warren, then the attorney general of California, wanted. But that is not what the Roosevelt administration did. It chose to steer a middle course between those who wanted no evacuation at all and those who, like Warren, wanted the Japanese-American population closely monitored. To call it an "internment" is at most a half-truth. . . .

The Second Question: Why Was It Done?

The nature of the military emergency. A situation of extreme military vulnerability existed in December 1941 and early 1942. The American Pacific Fleet, the United States' first line of defense in the Pacific, was destroyed by the December 7 Japanese attack on Pearl Harbor. The Japanese at the same time attacked Hong Kong, Malaysia, the Philippines, Wake and Midway Islands. The next day, they invaded Thailand. Within less than a week, Guam fell. By Christmas they had taken Wake Island and had occupied Hong Kong. Manila fell on January 2, and Singapore on February 10. The Battle of the Java Sea on February 27 resulted in a major Japanese naval victory. By early March Japan had control over Rangoon, Burma and the Netherlands East Indies. The struggle at Bataan and Corregidor marked the end of the

Japanese conquest of the Philippines. The Hawaiian Islands and the West Coast of the United States were unprotected from attack. On February 23 a Japanese submarine shelled an oil field along the California coast. Two days later five unidentified planes were spotted and Los Angeles underwent a black-out. The United States hurriedly made preparations for war. The extent of its unpreparedness is graphically illustrated by the draftees' use of wooden guns in their maneuvers in Louisiana in early 1942.

The substance of the charge of 'internment' is contradicted by the fact that resettlement outside the centers was diligently pursued.

Japanese exploitation of West Coast vulnerability. The critics of the evacuation often argue that there was no demonstrated military necessity for it. The [1982] Report of the Commission on Wartime Relocation [a presidential commission appointed to investigate U.S. relocation policy] speaks of "the clamor" by California officials for protective action, and says that "these opinions were not informed by any knowledge of actual military risks." The extensive critical literature mocks the perception of danger, suggesting that it was a figment of hysterical imaginations.

But this is nonsense. The danger was apparent to anyone who considered the situation. Earl Warren, as attorney general of California, testified before a select committee of Congress (the "Tolan Committee") on February 21, 1942, and submitted letters from a number of local officials. Some pointed to the vulnerability of the water supply and of the large-scale irrigation systems: "It would be absolutely humanly impossible," one of them wrote, "for the small force now available in the sheriff's office to make even a pretense of guarding this tremendous farm territory and the irrigation system." Another pointed out that "a systematic campaign of incendiarism would cause terrific disaster" during the California dry season from May until October. The city manager of Alameda observed that "we have the naval air station at one end of the island. . . . There are five major shipyards along the northern edge and there is the Oakland Airport at the eastern end of the island." Warren provided maps that showed that the

Japanese-American population lived in close proximity to virtually all strategic locations.

A situation of extreme military vulnerability existed in December 1941 and early 1942.

Many scenarios suggest themselves. Espionage, sabotage and aid to an invading army are obvious possibilities. To appreciate the danger we need a very real sense of what a terrible toll could have been exacted if even another Pearl Harbor had been committed. The potential, however, was for much more than that.

In addition to the civilian population, there was much that was important militarily and economically along the West Coast; it was clearly exposed; and there were few means to defend it. This was enough in itself to create a critical emergency, to be met as humanely but as effectively as possible. It should not be necessary for the American government to have known specifically of plans for espionage and sabotage.

Just the same, there *was* definitive evidence of Japan's intent to exploit (and actual exploitation of) the situation. On December 4, 1941, the Office of Naval Intelligence reported a Japanese "intelligence machine geared for war, in operation, and utilizing west coast Japanese." On January 21, 1942, a bulletin from Army Intelligence "stated flat out that the Japanese government's espionage net containing Japanese aliens, first and second generation Japanese and other nationals is now thoroughly organized and working underground," according to the [1984 Congressional] testimony of David D. Lowman, a retired career intelligence officer who has written extensively on declassified intelligence from World War II.

The Espionage Threat

The Commission on Wartime Relocation contradicted this in its 1982 Report when it said that "not a single documented act of espionage, sabotage or fifth column activity was committed by an American citizen of Japanese ancestry or by a resident Japanese alien on the West Coast." This claim is often repeated in the critical literature, but is blatantly false.

Amazingly, the Commission ignored the most important source of information about espionage, which is the dispatches sent by the Japanese government to its own officials before and during the war. U.S. Navy codebreakers had broken the Japanese diplomatic code in 1938, and the decoded messages were distributed, on a basis "higher than Top Secret," to a small handful of the very highest American officials under the codename "MAGIC." Lowman testified in 1984 that "included among the diplomatic communications were hundreds of reports dealing with espionage activities in the United States and its possessions. . . . In recruiting Japanese second generation and resident nationals, Tokyo warned to use the utmost caution. . . . In April [1941], Tokyo instructed all the consulates to wire home lists of first- and second-generation Japanese according to specified categories." The result, he said, was that "in May 1941, Japanese consulates on the west coast reported to Tokyo that first and second generation Japanese had been successfully recruited and were now spying on shipments of airplanes and war material in the San Diego and San Pedro areas. They were reporting on activities within aircraft plants in Seattle and Los Angeles. Local Japanese . . . were reporting on shipping activities at the Bremerton Naval Yard. . . . The Los Angeles consulate reported: 'We shall maintain connections with our second generation who are at present in the Army to keep us informed'. . . Seattle followed with a similar dispatch."

Several officials within the Roosevelt administration opposed the evacuation of the Japanese-Americans from the West Coast, but Lowman makes a telling point: that the President, the Secretary of War, the Army Chief of Staff, the Director of Military Intelligence, the Secretary of the Navy, the Chief of Naval Operations, the Director of Naval Intelligence, and the Chiefs of Army and Navy Plans—all of whom received MAGIC—*favored* evacuation. It was those who did not have knowledge of the Japanese dispatches who found it possible, somewhat incongruously in light of the self-evident factors I have mentioned, to doubt the military necessity.

Critics who damn the United States for the evacuation have sought to minimize the significance of MAGIC. John J. McCloy, who was Assistant Secretary of War during the war, testified in 1984 that "word has gone out now from the lobbyists to 'laugh off' the revelations of MAGIC."

The Commission on Wartime Relocation, established by Congress in 1980 and composed of such prominent figures as Arthur E. Goldberg, Arthur S. Flemming, Senator Edward Brooke, and Robert F. Drinan, didn't bother to laugh MAGIC off—it simply ignored it. . . .

The Japanese-American Community

The unassimilated nature of the Japanese-American community. The nature of the Japanese-American community on the West Coast at the time of World War II posed a dual problem. Because it was tightly-knit and unassimilated, it was attractive to Japan as a field for cultivation. At the same time, it was virtually impenetrable to efforts of the American government to sort out those whose loyalties were with Japan. . . .

The critics blame American caucasians for this lack of assimilation, pointing to the hostility that had been shown toward Asian immigrants by labor unions and others on the West Coast during the preceding decades. That, though, is another issue, one that asks whether it is wrong for the citizens of a country to oppose large-scale immigration by people who are considerably different from themselves. What is relevant to the question of the military emergency during World War II is not who was at fault for the Japanese-American community's lack of assimilation, but the uncontradicted fact that they were not assimilated. . . .

The Question of Loyalty

How loyal were the Japanese-Americans? This brings us to the most sensitive part of the study, since the "politically correct" thing to say is that *all* of the second-generation Japanese-Americans (the Nisei, who were the first to be born here, and even the Kibei, who were sent back to Japan for their education) were pro-American. I have already referred to Senator Hayakawa's sweeping generalization, which is bound to be appealing: "They had grown up loyal Americans." Accordingly, it is important to note again that it is no reflection on today's Americans of Japanese ancestry to take an honest look at what the situation was fifty years ago during World War II.

Many did strongly identify with the American side, and even distinguished themselves in combat on behalf of this country. An all-Nisei National Guard unit from Hawaii, the 100th Battalion, fought in Italy, winning much distinction, and was later merged into a newly-formed group, the 442nd [Regimental] Combat Team, which went on to fight in both Italy and France. . . .

To focus exclusively on this, however, obscures the truth, which taken as a whole was much more complex. Here are some aspects of that complexity:
• The War Relocation Authority had the evacuees fill out a questionnaire about their loyalty. Colonel Frederick Wiener testified [before Congress] in 1984 that "they asked first of the persons of military age whether they would serve in the Armed Forces of the United States; 94 percent of them gave negative answers. Now I will admit that it is asking a great deal of an individual after he is interned as a security risk [sic] to volunteer cheerfully for service. . . . I do not criticize it. What I criticize is that the 94 percent who didn't serve now wrap themselves in the regimental colors of the 442d RCT."
• A significant number sought repatriation to Japan. 9,028 applications were filed by the end of 1943, a total that swelled to 19,014 by a year later. Eventually, more than 16 percent of the evacuees asked for repatriation. Of these, 8,000 actually went back to Japan. In 1982 the Congressional Commission put the most favorable spin on this by blaming it on the evacuation: "No other statistics chronicle so clearly as these the decline of evacuees' faith in the United States." In any case, it runs clearly counter to the example set by those who served in the 442nd Combat Team.
• There was a powerful pro-Japan element within the relocation centers, forcing its members' eventual segregation into the facility at Tule Lake. Secretary of War Henry L. Stimson wrote in May 1943 about "a vicious, well-organized, pro-Japanese group to be found at each relocation center. Through agitation and violence, these groups gained control of many aspects of internal project administration, so much so that it became disadvantageous, and sometimes dangerous, to express loyalty to the United States." In the fall of 1942 some of the leaders of the Japanese American Citizens League were beaten by gangs after passing a resolution supporting the United States. Sometimes the pro-Japan element formed a competing system of center governance, electing its own block representatives. At the Manzanar center, a group called the Black Dragons championed Japan. . . .
• If Japan had invaded the West Coast, enormous pressures would have come to bear to support the invading army. Col. Bendetsen testified that wherever the Japanese invaded they

shot those of Japanese ancestry who did not embrace them
—and that this fact was well known. . . .

A Risky Decision

A question long-since forgotten: Was mere relocation a danger-
ously indulgent policy? Many officials on the West Coast and
in the western states wanted actual internment, not just relocation, for the duration of the war. Hindsight shows that
this wasn't necessary. As it turned out, the evacuation and
relocation worked well to protect both the national security
and the Japanese-Americans themselves.

It is easy to lose sight of the fact today, however, that the
decision not to intern them was made at great risk. Experience during the war did demonstrate that there were a sizeable number of Japanese-Americans who militantly supported Japan. If they had conducted even one massive act of
sabotage, would the risk have been worth it? How many
lives, say, was the risk worth? 100? 1,000? 10,000? Whose
lives?

The criticism of an inference. After the war began, authorities anticipated acts of sabotage on the West Coast—but
none occurred. Why? The critics of the evacuation argue
that this is evidence that there were no disloyal persons of
Japanese ancestry. A number of American officials at the
time, however, including Earl Warren, drew diametrically
the opposite inference: that there must be some who were
willing to commit sabotage, but that for some reason they
were being held back rather than being exposed. Warren
and the others, including the columnist Walter Lippmann,
considered it an ominous sign. This inference was later
ridiculed—in fact, called "vicious" and unprofessional—by
the Congressional Commission on Wartime Relocation.
Each reader should be able to decide for himself whether
the reasoning was flawed (and, for those who agree with the
critics who say that it was, whether it can appropriately be
characterized as vicious).

A critically important choice: Mass evacuation or a case-by-
case loyalty determination. The normal course of law in a legal system that respects individual rights looks at the guilt
of individuals, providing each "due process." The critics of
the evacuation invoke this as the ground for a bitter de-
nunciation of American policy, since the policy treated the
Japanese-Americans as a group. The critical view would

follow almost naturally from a position that acknowledges virtually no need for protective measures in the emergency: If the threat were slight, it would hardly outweigh the important value to be given to individual due process. We have already seen, however, that there *was* a vital need for immediate action.

There were a sizeable number of Japanese-Americans who militantly supported Japan.

The critical view would also be reasonable if the American government had had an expeditious way to determine, by investigation and hearings, the loyalty of each person on an individual basis. But this was a virtual impossibility, given the cultural insularity of the Japanese-American community. (To make any practical sense, it presupposes that many of the Japanese-Americans would have come forward in hearings as witnesses against other Japanese-Americans; but we have seen the internal pressures, including murderous beatings, that the pro-Japan element could have brought to bear against it.). . .

Other Questions

Why wasn't the same done with the Hawaiian Japanese-Americans? The point is sometimes made that the evacuation from the West Coast was inconsistent with having left the Japanese-American population on Hawaii. The answer is that with the declaration of martial law and the suspension of the writ of habeas corpus in December 1941, Hawaii was placed under direct military control. . . . This was not done on the mainland.

Why weren't Americans of German and Italian extraction evacuated? Another point of criticism asks why the Japanese-Americans were evacuated but people of German and Italian ancestry were not. This has a double edge: it suggests that the evacuation really wasn't necessary; and it suggests that the evacuation was racially motivated.

Senator Hayakawa wrote that "the answer is obvious. Germans and Italians, having come to America earlier than the Japanese and in far greater numbers, were already well-known to Americans in 1941." The same point was expressed in a letter that the city officials of Madera, California, wrote to then-attorney general Earl Warren in early 1942: "The general feeling about the Italians is that they are well assimilated, and we do not regard even the Italian aliens alien in fact. . . . So far as we know, there are no German aliens in this community." The distinction lies in the vast difference in assimilation. The Germans and Italians had long-since become mixed with the general population. . . .

Was the relocation a product of "racism"? Much public opinion on the West Coast had long been hostile to Japanese and other Asian immigration. Organized labor was for many years prominent among its opponents. And there is no question but that public opinion was inflamed against the Japanese during World War II, especially immediately following Pearl Harbor. This feeling was most intense on the West Coast, for a very specific reason: the National Guard units from eleven western states were fighting in the Philippines, where they were tortured and starved by their Japanese captors. Their families and friends felt passionately about these atrocities.

One of the motivating factors in the policy of evacuation and resettlement was to protect the Japanese-Americans from public anger.

Throughout the war, one of the motivating factors in the policy of evacuation and resettlement was to protect the Japanese-Americans from public anger. It is easy today to say that that anger was "racist," but we have reason to be suspicious of attitudes taken under much more comfortable circumstances forty and even fifty years after the fact. To argue that the anger was vicious has, itself, a certain vicious quality about it.

There were ample reasons for the evacuation that had nothing to do with racism. Justice Hugo Black wrote levelheadedly about this in 1944 [*Korematsu v. United States*]: "To cast this case into outlines of racial prejudice, without reference to the real military dangers which were present, merely confuses the issue. Korematsu was not excluded from the Military Area because of hostility to him or his race. . . . He *was* excluded because we are at war with the Japanese Empire.". . .

Complex Circumstances

The circumstances during World War II were much more complicated than those who would damn the United States as having "viciously set up concentration camps for the Japanese-Americans" ever admit. My study of the subject has persuaded me that Americans have nothing to be ashamed of about this episode, even though it is regrettable that war and its incidents ever have to happen. We should, however, be ashamed of the way in which we as a people have wallowed in self-abasement in our eagerness to be "generous" and "sensitive" in response to the bitter censures of alienated ideology. Most Americans I have talked with are thoroughly uninformed as to what actually happened and why, and yet are eager to join in the condemnation of the actions of the United States.

Chapter **2**

Constitutional Questions Raised by the Treatment of Japanese Americans

1

Supreme Court Justices Disagree on Japanese-American Evacuation

Part I: Hugo Black; Part II: Frank Murphy

Korematsu v. United States was one of several cases brought before the U.S. Supreme Court during World War II challenging the constitutionality of U.S. policy toward Japanese Americans. In a previous case, *Hirabayashi v. United States*, the Supreme Court in June 1943 unanimously upheld military curfews restricting the movement of Japanese Americans as a necessary war measure. Eighteen months later in December 1944, a divided Supreme Court upheld the constitutionality of the mass evacuation of Japanese Americans in *Korematsu*.

Fred Korematsu was a San Francisco area resident who refused to comply with a military order calling for all people of Japanese descent to evacuate that area. He was arrested by the police, convicted in a federal court of violating Public Law 503 (which made it a federal crime to disobey military orders such as the evacuation rule), and sentenced to five years probation. Although the sentence did not include jail, Korematsu was detained in the Tanforan assembly center along with other Japanese Americans. His conviction was appealed to the U.S. Court of Appeals and ultimately to the Supreme Court, which heard oral arguments in October 1944. The Court delivered its decision on December 18, 1944. Passages from the majority opinion and one minority opinion are excerpted here.

Hugo Black, a Supreme Court justice from 1937 to 1971, wrote the majority opinion in the 6-3 decision upholding the constitutionality of Koramatsu's conviction and the mass exclusion order. Citing the *Hirabayashi* case, Black concludes that al-

Part I: Reprinted from the majority opinion, written by Hugo Black, in the U.S. Supreme Court case of *Korematsu v. United States*, December 18, 1944. *Part II:* From the dissenting opinion, written by Frank Murphy, in *Korematsu v. United States*.

though civil rights restrictions based on race are "immediately suspect," wartime security concerns justify military orders for the mass exclusion of Japanese Americans. Frank Murphy, who served on the Supreme Court from 1940 to 1949, was one of three justices to issue dissenting opinions. He charges that mass exclusion orders result in a racist and unjustifiable abridgement of the constitutional rights of Korematsu and other Japanese Americans.

I

Hugo Black's majority opinion in *Korematsu v. United States*

The petitioner, an American citizen of Japanese descent, was convicted in a federal district court for remaining in San Leandro, California, a "Military Area," contrary to Civilian Exclusion Order No. 34 of the Commanding General of the Western Command, U.S. Army, which directed that after May 9, 1942, all persons of Japanese ancestry should be excluded from that area. No question was raised as to petitioner's loyalty to the United States. The Circuit Court of Appeals affirmed, and the importance of the constitutional question involved caused us to grant certiorari.

It should be noted, to begin with, that all legal restrictions which curtail the civil rights of a single racial group are immediately suspect. That is not to say that all such restrictions are unconstitutional. It is to say that courts must subject them to the most rigid scrutiny. Pressing public necessity may sometimes justify the existence of such restrictions; racial antagonism never can. . . .

War Powers

The 1942 Act was attacked in the *Hirabayashi* case as an unconstitutional delegation of power; it was contended that the curfew order and other orders on which it rested were beyond the war powers of the Congress, the military authorities and of the President, as Commander in Chief of the Army; and finally that to apply the curfew order against none but citizens of Japanese ancestry amounted to a constitutionally prohibited discrimination solely on account of race. To these questions, we gave the serious consideration which their importance justified. We upheld the curfew order as an exercise of the power of the government to take steps necessary to prevent espionage and sabotage in an area threatened by Japanese attack.

In the light of the principles we announced in the *Hirabayashi* case, we are unable to conclude that it was beyond the war power of Congress and the Executive to exclude those of Japanese ancestry from the West Coast war area at the time they did. True, exclusion from the area in which one's home is located is a far greater deprivation than constant confinement to the home from 8 p.m. to 6 a.m. Nothing short of apprehension by the proper military authorities of the gravest imminent danger to the public safety can constitutionally justify either. But exclusion from a threatened area, no less than curfew, has a definite and close relationship to the prevention of espionage and sabotage. The military authorities, charged with the primary responsibility of defending our shores, concluded that curfew provided inadequate protection and ordered exclusion. They did so, as pointed out in our *Hirabayashi* opinion, in accordance with Congressional authority to the military to say who should, and who should not, remain in the threatened areas.

In this case the petitioner challenges the assumptions upon which we rested our conclusions in the *Hirabayashi* case. He also urges that by May 1942, when Order No. 34 was promulgated, all danger of Japanese invasion of the West Coast had disappeared. After careful consideration of these contentions we are compelled to reject them.

Here, as in the *Hirabayashi* case, *supra*, p. 99, ". . . we cannot reject as unfounded the judgment of the military authorities and of Congress that there were disloyal members of that population, whose number and strength could not be precisely and quickly ascertained. We cannot say that the war-making branches of the Government did not have ground for believing that in a critical hour such persons could not readily be isolated and separately dealt with, and constituted a menace to the national defense and safety, which demanded that prompt and adequate measures be taken to guard against it."

Like curfew, exclusion of those of Japanese origin was deemed necessary because of the presence of an unascertained number of disloyal members of the group, most of whom we have no doubt were loyal to this country. It was because we could not reject the finding of the military authorities that it was impossible to bring about an immediate segregation of the disloyal from the loyal that we sustained the validity of the curfew order as applying to the whole group. In the instant case, temporary exclusion of the entire group was rested by the military on the same ground. The judgment that exclusion of the whole group was for the same reason a military imperative answers the contention that the exclusion was in the nature of group punishment based on antagonism to those of Japanese origin. That there were members of the group who retained loyalties to Japan has been confirmed by investigations made subsequent to the exclusion. Approximately five thousand American citizens of Japanese ancestry refused to swear unqualified allegiance to the United States and to renounce allegiance to the Japanese Emperor, and several thousand evacuees requested repatriation to Japan.

The Burdens of Citizenship

We uphold the exclusion order as of the time it was made and when the petitioner violated it. . . . In doing so, we are not unmindful of the hardships imposed by it upon a large group of American citizens. . . . But hardships are part of war and war is an aggregation of hardships. All citizens alike, both in and out of uniform, feel the impact of war in greater or lesser measure. Citizenship has its responsibilities as well as its privileges, and in time of war the burden is always heavier. Compulsory exclusion of large groups of citizens from their homes, except under circumstances of direst emergency and peril, is inconsistent with our basic governmental institutions. But when under conditions of modern warfare our shores are threatened by hostile forces, the power to protect must be commensurate with the threatened danger. . . .

Hardships are part of war.

It is said that we are dealing here with the case of imprisonment of a citizen in a concentration camp solely because of his ancestry, without evidence or inquiry concerning his loyalty and good disposition towards the United States. Our task would be simple, our duty clear, were this a case involving the imprisonment of a loyal citizen in a concentration camp because of racial prejudice. Regardless of the true nature of the assembly and relocation centers—and we deem it unjustifiable to call them concentration camps with all the ugly connotations that term implies—we are dealing specifically with nothing but an exclusion order. To cast this case into outlines of racial prejudice, without reference to the real military dangers which were presented, merely confuses the issue. Korematsu was not excluded from the Military Area because of hostility to him or his race. He *was* excluded because we are at war with the Japanese Empire, because the properly constituted military authorities feared an invasion of our West Coast and felt constrained to take proper security measures, because they decided that the military urgency of the situation demanded that all citizens of Japanese ancestry be segregated from the West Coast temporarily, and finally, because Congress, reposing its confidence in this time of war in our military leaders—as inevitably it must—determined that they should have the power to do just this. There was evidence of disloyalty on the part of some, the military authorities considered that the need for action was great, and time was short. We cannot—by availing ourselves of the calm perspective of hindsight—now say that at that time these actions were unjustified.

II

Frank Murphy's dissenting opinion in *Korematsu v. United States*

This exclusion of "all persons of Japanese ancestry, both alien and non-alien," from the Pacific Coast area on a plea of military necessity in the absence of martial law ought not to be approved. Such exclusion goes over "the very brink of constitutional power" and falls into the ugly abyss of racism.

In dealing with matters relating to the prosecution and progress of a war, we must accord great respect and consideration to the judgments of the military authorities who are on the scene and who have full knowledge of the military facts. The scope of their discretion must, as a matter of necessity and common sense, be wide. And their judgments ought not to be overruled lightly by those whose training and duties ill-quip them to deal intelligently with matters so vital to the physical security of the nation.

At the same time, however, it is essential that there be definite limits to military discretion, especially where martial law has not been declared. . . .

Violating Constitutional Rights

The judicial test of whether the Government, on a plea of military necessity, can validly deprive an individual of any of his constitutional rights is whether the deprivation is reasonably related to a public danger that is so "immediate, imminent, and impending" as not to admit of delay and not to permit the intervention of ordinary constitutional processes to alleviate the danger. . . . Civilian Exclusion Order No. 34, banishing from a prescribed area of the Pacific Coast "all persons of Japanese ancestry, both alien and non-alien," clearly does not meet that test. Being an obvious racial discrimination, the order deprives all those within its scope of the equal protection of the laws as guaranteed by the Fifth Amendment. It further deprives these individuals of their constitutional rights to live and work where they will, to establish a home where they choose and to move about freely. In excommunicating them without benefit of hearings, this order also deprives them of all their constitutional rights to procedural due process. Yet no reasonable relation to an "immediate, imminent, and impending" public danger is evident to support this racial restriction which is one of the most sweeping and complete deprivations of constitutional rights in the history of this nation in the absence of martial law.

To cast this case into outlines of racial prejudice, without reference to the real military dangers which were presented, merely confuses the issue.

It must be conceded that the military and naval situation in the spring of 1942 was such as to generate a very real fear of invasion of the Pacific Coast, accompanied by fears of sabotage and espionage in that area. The military command was therefore justified in adopting all reasonable means necessary to combat these dangers. In adjudging the military action taken in light of the then apparent dangers, we must not erect too high or too meticulous standards; it is necessary only that the action have some reasonable relation to the removal of the dangers of invasion, sabotage and espionage. But the exclusion, either temporarily or permanently, of all persons with Japanese blood in their veins has no such reasonable relation. And that relation is lacking because the exclusion order necessarily must rely for its reasonableness upon the assumption that *all* persons of Japanese ancestry may have a dangerous tendency to commit sabotage and espionage and to aid our Japanese enemy in other ways. It is difficult to believe that reason, logic or experience could be marshalled in support of such an assumption.

This forced exclusion was the result in good measure of . . . [an] erroneous assumption of racial guilt rather than bona fide military necessity.

That this forced exclusion was the result in good measure of this erroneous assumption of racial guilt rather than bona fide military necessity is evidenced by the Commanding General's Final Report on the evacuation from the Pacific Coast area. In it he refers to all individuals of Japanese descent as "subversive," as belonging to "an enemy race" whose "racial strains are undiluted," and as constituting "over 112,000 potential enemies . . . at large today" along the Pacific Coast. In support of this blanket condemnation of all persons of Japanese descent, however, no reliable evidence is cited to show that such individuals were generally disloyal, or had generally so conducted themselves in this area as to constitute a special menace to defense installations or war industries, or had otherwise by their behavior furnished reasonable ground for their exclusion as a group.

Racial Prejudice

Justification for the exclusion is sought, instead, mainly upon questionable racial and sociological grounds not ordinarily within the realm of expert military judgment, supplemented by certain semi-military conclusions drawn from an unwarranted use of circumstantial evidence. Individuals of Japanese ancestry are condemned because they are said to be "a large, unassimilated, tightly knit racial group, bound to an enemy nation by strong ties of race, culture, custom and religion." They are claimed to be given to "emperor worshipping ceremonies" and to "dual citizenship." Japanese language schools and allegedly pro-Japanese organizations are cited as evidence of possible group disloyalty, together with facts as to certain persons being educated and residing at length in Japan. It is intimated that many of these individuals deliberately resided "adjacent to strategic points," thus enabling them "to carry into execution a tremendous program of sabotage on a mass scale should any considerable number of them have been inclined to do so." . . . Finally, it is intimated, though not directly charged or proved, that persons of Japanese ancestry were responsible for three minor isolated shellings and bombings of the Pacific Coast area, as well as for unidentified radio transmissions and night signalling.

The main reasons relied upon by those responsible for the forced evacuation, therefore, do not prove a reasonable relation between the group characteristics of Japanese Americans and the dangers of invasion, sabotage and espionage. The reasons appear, instead, to be largely an accumulation of much of the misinformation, half-truths and insinuations that for years have been directed against Japanese Americans by people with racial and economic prejudices— the same people who have been among the foremost advocates of the evacuation. A military judgment based upon such racial and sociological considerations is not entitled to the great weight ordinarily given the judgments based upon strictly military considerations. Especially is this so when every charge relative to race, religion, culture, geographical location, and legal and economic status has been substantially discredited by independent studies made by experts in these matters. . . .

No adequate reason is given for the failure to treat these Japanese Americans on an individual basis by holding investigations and hearings to separate the loyal from the disloyal, as was done in the case of persons of German and Italian ancestry. . . . It is asserted merely that the loyalties of this group "were unknown and time was of the essence." Yet nearly four months elapsed after Pearl Harbor before the first exclusion order was issued; nearly eight months went by until the last order was issued; and the last of these "subversive" persons was not actually removed until almost eleven months had elapsed. Leisure and deliberation seem to have been more of the essence than speed. And the fact that conditions were not such as to warrant a declaration of martial law adds strength to the belief that the factors of time and military necessity were not as urgent as they have been represented to be.

I dissent . . . from this legalization of racism.

Moreover, there was no adequate proof that the Federal Bureau of Investigation and the military and naval intelligence services did not have the espionage and sabotage situation well in hand during this long period. Nor is there any denial of the fact that not one person of Japanese ancestry was accused or convicted of espionage or sabotage after Pearl Harbor while they were still free, a fact which is some evidence of the loyalty of the vast majority of these individuals and of the effectiveness of the established methods of combatting these evils. It seems incredible that under these circumstances it would have been impossible to hold loyalty hearings for the mere 112,000 persons involved—or at least for the 70,000 American citizens—especially when a large part of this number represented children and elderly men and women. . . .

All Americans Have Equal Constitutional Rights

I dissent, therefore, from this legalization of racism. Racial discrimination in any form and in any degree has no justifiable part whatever in our democratic way of life. It is unattractive in any setting but it is utterly revolting among a free people who have embraced the principles set forth in the Constitution of the United States. All residents of this nation are kin in some way by blood or culture to a foreign land. Yet they are primarily and necessarily a part of the new and distinct civilization of the United States. They must accordingly be treated at all times as the heirs of the American experiment and as entitled to all the rights and freedoms guaranteed by the Constitution.

2

How Disputed Evidence Affected the *Korematsu* Case

David M. Kennedy

Historian David M. Kennedy examines some of the arguments and maneuverings involved in the Supreme Court cases concerning the World War II internment of Japanese Americans. He focuses especially on the case involving Fred Korematsu, an American-born citizen of Japanese immigrant parents who was arrested and convicted for violating the evacuation order calling for all Japanese Americans to leave the West Coast. Kennedy argues that the United States government was itself divided on the issue, with members of the Justice and War departments at odds over what evidence should be presented to the Supreme Court. He argues that the Supreme Court may have been persuaded to overturn mass evacuation as unconstitutional if evidence questioning its military necessity had been presented. Kennedy, a history professor at Stanford University, is the author of *Freedom from Fear: The American People in Depression and War, 1929–1945*, from which the following passage was excerpted.

War Department officials watched anxiously as several lawsuits challenging the constitutionality of the relocation scheme made their way through the courts. On June 21, 1943, the Supreme Court ruled unanimously in the government's favor in the first two cases, though both turned on technicalities that allowed the Court to evade a decision on the central issues of coerced evacuation and compulsory internment. In one of those cases, *Hirabayashi v. United States,* Justice Frank Murphy's concurring opinion sounded an ominous warning. The relocation program, he admonished, ventured perilously close "to the very brink of constitutional power." For the first time in history, Murphy wrote, the Court had "sustained a substantial restriction of the personal liberty of citizens of the United States based upon the accident of race or ancestry." The government's policy, he darkly concluded, bore, "a melancholy resemblance to the treatment accorded to members of the Jewish race in Germany and in other parts of Europe."

Korematsu was an unlikely paragon of his sorely abused people.

Of the remaining suits, Fred Korematsu's held the greatest threat to the constitutionality of the relocation program. Korematsu was an unlikely paragon of his sorely abused people. A twenty-three-year-old American-born Nisei living in the San Francisco Bay area in the spring of 1942, he had a good welding job and an Italian-American fiancée, and no wish to leave either. When [Gen. John] DeWitt issued his evacuation order, Korematsu forged his identity papers, underwent plastic surgery to change his facial appearance, and prepared to wait out the war as a "Spanish-Hawaiian" named "Clyde Sarah." The subterfuge came to an inglorious end on the afternoon of May 30, 1942, when police acting on a tip arrested Korematsu as he was strolling down a street with his girlfriend in San Leandro, California. An American Civil Liberties Union lawyer read of the arrest in the newspaper, visited Korematsu in jail, and asked if he would allow his case to be used as a test of the evacuation decree. Somewhat surprisingly, Korematsu agreed.

DeWitt's Final Report

While Korematsu's case began its slow journey through the legal system, DeWitt's deputy Colonel Karl R. Bendetsen was drafting a document for DeWitt's signature entitled *Final Report, Japanese Evacuation from the West Coast, 1942.* Ten months in preparation, 618 pages long, it offered DeWitt's official explanation for what he had done: "military necessity." Justice Department lawyers first saw the report in January 1944, as they were preparing their briefs in the Korematsu case. What they read stunned them. The *Final Report* ignited an uproar that raged for eight months, a donnybrook between the Justice and War departments that ended with a pathetic but constitutionally fateful whimper in a last-ditch skirmish over a three-sentence footnote.

To buttress the argument that forced evacuation was a matter of military necessity, Bendetsen had laced the *Final Report* with hundreds of examples of subversive activities on the West Coast in the winter and spring of 1942. That evidence was the indispensable basis for the government's claim that its relocation program lay within constitutional bounds. But the Justice Department lawyers quickly saw that Bendetsen had cooked his facts. His statement that an FBI raid had turned up "more than 60,000 rounds of ammunition and many rifles, shotguns and maps," for example, failed to mention that those items had come from a sporting-goods store. Worse, when Biddle asked the FBI and the Federal Communications Commission (FCC) to review the report's charges, the responses were unequivocal. [FBI director J. Edgar] Hoover replied that "there is no information in the possession of this Bureau" that supported Bendetsen's claims about espionage. The FCC's response was even more damning. Citing its own 1942 study that had shown DeWitt's claims about supposedly illicit radio transmissions to be false, the FCC expressed its outrage that the allegations had resurfaced in the report. "There wasn't a single illicit station and DeWitt knew it," an FCC technician said.

A Controversial Footnote

Armed with these findings, Justice Department attorneys determined to disavow the *Final Report* in their presentation of the *Korematsu* case. Excluding the evidence in the report—in legal language, instructing the Court to take no judicial notice of it—would fatally undermine the factual basis for the argument that military necessity justified the violation of Fred Korematsu's constitutional right to live where he pleased. To that end, the department's drafting team carefully tamped a high-explosive footnote into its brief:

> The Final Report of General DeWitt is relied on in
> this brief for statistics and other details concerning the

actual evacuation and the events that took place subsequent thereto. The recital of the circumstances justifying the evacuation as a matter of military necessity, however, is in several respects, particularly with reference to the use of illegal radio transmitters and to shore-to-ship signaling by persons of Japanese ancestry, in conflict with information in the possession of the Department of Justice. In view of the contrariety of the reports on this matter we do not ask the Court to take judicial notice of the recital of those facts contained in the Report.

Privately, the lawyers used less measured language. The report's allegations of espionage, sabotage, and treason, they said, were "lies." Propagating these intentional falsehoods was "highly unfair to this racial minority." Left uncorrected, the report would mean that "the whole historical record of this matter will be as the military choose to state it."

The footnote detonated in Assistant Secretary of War [John J.] McCloy's hands when he read a draft of the Justice Department's brief on Saturday morning, September 30, 1944. McCloy reflexively understood that its effect would be to explode the shaky consensus the Court had patched together in the *Hirabayashi* case, and probably to induce a judgment that the entire relocation program was unconstitutional. He insisted that the damning footnote be amended. After two days of frantic argument, the top officials at the Justice Department once again buckled under McCloy's pressure and deleted the offending footnote. Ignorant of this dispute, the Supreme Court justices proceeded to deliberate on the *Korematsu* case deprived of a basis on which to challenge the factual assertions of the *Final Report*.

The *Korematsu* Decision

Even so, the Court was clearly queasy about the *Korematsu* case. Justice Hugo Black's majority opinion upheld Fred Korematsu's original conviction for violating the evacuation decree while carefully avoiding any pronouncement on the legality of his subsequent internment. "All legal restrictions which curtail the civil rights of a single racial group are immediately suspect," Black cautioned, and must be subjected to the strictest scrutiny. But military necessity, Black concluded, provided sufficient grounds to believe that the government's actions passed the strict scrutiny test in Korematsu's case. Justices [Owen] Roberts, [Frank] Murphy, and [Robert H.] Jackson dissented. Jackson objected that the Court had "validated the principle of racial discrimination." If McCloy had not succeeded in expunging the footnote that called DeWitt's *Final Report* into question, a majority of the Court would quite possibly have found in Korematsu's favor. As it was, though no racially restrictive law has ever since passed the strict scrutiny test, the *Korematsu* precedent, in Jackson's phrase, "lies about like a loaded weapon ready for the hand of any authority that can bring forward a plausible claim to an urgent need."

The Court was clearly queasy about the Korematsu *case.*

When the Court pronounced on the *Korematsu* case on December 18, 1944, safely after the November presidential election, the camps had already begun to empty. Just the day before the Court's decision was announced, the government had declared that the period of "military necessity" was ended. West Coast military authorities rescinded DeWitt's original evacuation order and restored to the remaining camp residents "their full rights to enter and remain in the military areas of the Western Defense Command."

The sorry history of Korematsu's bowdlerized brief condemns the Court's ruling as a judicial travesty. For the Japanese internees, the entire episode had been a cruel torment. By one estimate they suffered some $400 million in property losses as a result of evacuation. Congress in 1948 provided a paltry $37 million in reparations. In another spasm of conscience forty years later, Congress awarded $20,000 to each surviving detainee. President Bill Clinton rendered further atonement in 1998 when he bestowed the nation's highest civilian honor, the Presidential Medal of Freedom, on that implausible paladin, Fred Korematsu.

3

The Supreme Court's Dismal Failure to Protect Constitutional Rights

Jacobus tenBroek, Edward N. Barnhart, and Floyd W. Matson

The Supreme Court's decisions concerning Japanese-American internment have been, in hindsight, criticized by many. One such critic was Jacobus tenBroek, a professor of speech and political science at the University of California at Berkeley and the author of numerous works on constitutional law. He collaborated with political scholars Edward N. Barnhart and Floyd W. Matson to write *Prejudice, War, and the Constitution*, the third volume of the Japanese Evacuation and Resettlement Study (JERS), a social sciences project sponsored and coordinated by the University of California. The book focused on the history, causes, and legal implications of Japanese-American evacuation. tenBroek was the primary author of the book's conclusion, excerpted here. He argues that the mass relocation and internment of Japanese Americans was a disgraceful episode in which the U.S. government deprived Japanese Americans of their civil rights. He faults the Supreme Court for failing to recognize the threat the government's actions posed to civil liberties for all Americans.

Viewed in the perspective of a decade, with all the advantages of hindsight and subsequent disclosure, the Japanese American episode of World War II looms as a great and evil blotch upon our national history. The whole vast, harsh, and discriminatory program of uprooting and imprisonment—initiated by the generals, advised, ordered, and supervised by the civilian heads of the War Department, authorized by the President, implemented by Congress, approved by the Supreme Court, and supported by the people—is without parallel in our past and full of ominous forebodings for our future.

The Japanese American episode of World War II looms as a great and evil blotch upon our national history.

The entire Japanese American program violated and degraded the basic individualism which sustains a democracy. It impaired the trial tradition of the common law. It disparaged the principle that guilt is individual. It sapped the vitality of the precept of equality. It made racism a constitutional principle. It tolerated preventive incarceration for assumed disloyal beliefs and attitudes—unaccompanied by acts—attributing them without proof, probable cause, or reasonable suspicion to an entire group on a basis of race. Recklessly and unnecessarily, it loosened judicial control of the military and produced dangerous imbalance in our government.

The episode embodied one of the most "sweeping and complete deprivations of constitutional rights in the history of this nation" [from Justice Frank Murphy's dissent in *Korematsu v. United States*]. It destroyed basic and precious rights of personal security: the right—without arbitrary or constitutionally irrelevant interference—to move about freely, to live and work where one chooses, to establish and maintain a home; the right not to be deprived of constitutional safeguards except upon an individual basis and after charges, notice, hearing, fair trial, and all of the procedural requirements of due process. It destroyed, as well, basic and precious rights of democratic participation: the right of peaceable assembly to discuss the general welfare and problems of government; the rights of free speech and a free press; the right freely to hear, read, and learn; the rights of petition and remonstrance; the rights of franchise and election, of seeking and holding office; and, not least of all, the right and responsibility to defend one's native land, if need be with one's life.

The Japanese American episode culminated in a constitutional sanctification of these deprivations by the highest court in the land—a court dedicated to justice, defense of the Constitution, determination of the powers and limitations of government, and protection of the rights of men.

Historical Perspective

In the historical view, the wisdom of a decision is tested principally by subsequent events. Contemporary plausibility is only a minor criterion. Judged by the historical test, military necessity arising out of the war emergency does not provide justification of the program of removal and imprisonment. It is true that Japanese arms, in the winter of 1941–42, advanced rapidly in southeast Asia and the southwest Pacific. Damaging blows were dealt the American navy. A foothold was gained on Attu and Kiska in the Aleutians, Dutch Harbor in Alaska was bombed. But it is also true that Japanese strength had been fully committed in the far Pacific. The mainland Pacific coastline of the United States was adequately protected even before December was out. The Battle of Midway on June 6, 1942, brought Japanese naval expansion in the Pacific to an end. Thereafter, the enemy forces on Attu and Kiska withered from lack of support.

There was no invasion of the coastal mainland. There were not even commando raids or air strikes upon it. One submarine lobbed a few shells harmlessly near an oil installation not far from Santa Barbara (February 23, 1942). Another sent a midget airplane with an incendiary bomb over an Oregon forest (September 9, 1942); the bomb ignited nothing. A third submarine fired on coast defenses at Astoria, Oregon (June 21, 1942). In December, 1941, there were only three successful enemy submarine attacks on ships leaving West Coast ports. In January, 1942, there were none; in February none; in March none; in April none; in May none. No Japanese surface ship ever operated in the eastern part of the Pacific between Hawaii and the mainland.

Thus, in the calm retrospect of history, it is evident that military necessity warranting the program simply did not exist. After Midway, there was no justification at all for either mass detention or mass exclusion. Even before Midway, there was no justification for mass detention or for the mass exclusion of American citizens of Japanese ancestry. There was no justification at any time for treating Japanese aliens differently from other enemy aliens.

The absence of any acts of espionage and sabotage by

Japanese Americans between Pearl Harbor and evacuation—while numerous persons of other extractions were being convicted of such acts—sufficiently testifies (1) to the active or passive loyalty of the major part of the Japanese American population, and (2) to the adequacy of existing methods of control and prevention. Even were this not so, alternative methods of control were available, less drastic than evacuation and detention combined or than either of them separately, more consonant with the Constitution and wholly adequate to meet the actual danger.

What Military Leaders Knew

All this can now be seen clearly. But even if we abandon the vantage point of history and judge the military only by what they then knew, the same conclusion must be reached. For the fact is that much of what was learned by the public only years later was, at the time, known to our military leaders. It was their judgment then that Japanese strength had been fully committed elsewhere; that, after December, the Pacific Coast was adequately protected. They knew the Japanese strength on land, sea, and in the air. They knew where it was deployed and what its capabilities were. The Navy especially believed that invasion was virtually out of the question by the spring of 1942. The significance of Midway was correctly appraised at the time. Yet it was after that battle that the inland Japanese Americans were evacuated and all Japanese Americans removed from assembly centers to relocation centers.

> *In the calm retrospect of history, it is evident that military necessity warranting the program simply did not exist.*

The weakness of the case for military necessity was spotlighted rather than concealed by General [John] DeWitt's *Final Report*, which is a flimsy tissue of misstatements, preposterous absurdities, patently fallacious reasoning, unacknowledged quotations, and uses facts and arguments developed after the event in an obvious attempt to show that, at the time the decision for evacuation was made, it was based on facts and sound reasoning. Most remarkable of all are these two assertions, contained in a single paragraph: "The very fact that no sabotage has taken place to date is a disturbing and confirming indication that such action will be taken"; and "The Japanese race is an enemy race and while many second and third generation Japanese born on United States soil, possessed of United States citizenship, have become 'Americanized,' the racial strains are undiluted.". . . .

To portray General DeWitt as the sole or even the chief villain in this tragic drama, as has so often been done, is as much an injustice as to absolve him altogether. . . .

President Roosevelt's Role

Even greater responsibility rests upon President Franklin D. Roosevelt and his civilian aides in the War Department, Secretary Henry L. Stimson and Assistant Secretary John J. McCloy, and upon the Congress of the United States. General DeWitt did not order evacuation and incarceration independently and without prior authorization from his superiors. We do not have here the imaginary problem, posed by Justice [Robert H.] Jackson in his *Korematsu* dissent, of an "irresponsible" and "unscrupulous" commander refusing to submit to higher civil authority. What we have, on the contrary, is a commander who proceeded meticulously through duly constituted channels. He presented his plan and request for authority to the War Department, thence to the President, and eventually to Congress. In response, the President, as the President alone could, issued Executive Order 9066, fully empowering the Secretary of War to put the proposed plan into operation. Thereafter, and pursuant to this delegation of authority, Secretary Henry L. Stimson, the civilian head of the War Department, and John J. McCloy, his civilian assistant, first modified the plan by exempting German and Italian American citizens and aliens, then ordered it put into effect, and, finally, continuously supervised its execution. Meanwhile, the Congress of the United States duly enacted Public Law 503, encompassing and providing civilian sanctions for Executive Order 9066 and the sub-delegations under it.

Thus, for these days which in their own way will live in infamy, President Roosevelt bears a large share of the responsibility. He bears it not only in the inert and formal sense that he was the chief executive of the nation and hence accountable for the acts of his subordinates whether he knew of them or not, but also in the immediate and active sense that he deliberately and knowingly authorized the program through the issuance of Executive Order 9066, thereafter supplemented it by other executive orders, and personally directed that its termination be delayed until after the presidential election of 1944. The action of Congress was also taken after due consideration. The President and the Congress of the United States were in fact, as well as in every proper constitutional and democratic sense, the agencies of ultimate decision. That their decision conformed to popular clamor and a request from the military does not and cannot relieve them of ultimate responsibility.

McCloy's apologetic statement that "the military men made the decision—it was a military decision" may indicate the attitude of the Washington officials involved in the decision. It does not and it cannot, however, explain the failure of McCloy and of Secretary Stimson to perform the function implicit in the historic purpose behind the requirement that the War Department must have civilian heads.

The Supreme Court's Failure

Responsibility rests, finally, with the courts, and especially with the Supreme Court of the United States. In many ways the failure of the Supreme Court was the greatest failure of all. For the military is preoccupied with war, not with the Constitution and men's rights. The President and Congress, too, are "war-waging" branches of government. The primary action and affirmative decision was theirs; but they moved on the brink of the event when the general course and outcome of the war were altogether uncertain. In 1945 General [George C.] Marshall pointed out that in "the black days of 1942 when the Japanese conquered all of Malaysia, occupied Burma, and threatened India while the German armies approached the Volga and the Suez . . . Germany and Japan came so close to complete domination of the world that we do not yet realize how thin the thread of Allied survival had been stretched."

In many ways the failure of the Supreme Court was the greatest failure of all.

Among the branches of government, the Supreme Court occupies a unique position. It is not so much an active as a reflective body. Its decisions are made on the nether side of the event. Its job is not primary but secondary. It is the historian of events as much as it is their maker. It exerts only such constructive leadership as derives from the power to negate the policy of others. Its self-arrogated and perhaps inherent function is to strike the governmental balance between motion and stability, between new action and old doctrines, between the powers of the nation and men's rights.

If the court had struck down the program, the Japanese American episode would have lived in history as nothing worse than a military blunder.

If the court had struck down the program, the Japanese American episode would have lived in history as nothing worse than a military blunder. But the court approved the program as constitutional, a step with implications and consequences accurately described by Justice Jackson in his dissenting opinion on the *Korematsu* case:

> Much is said of the danger to liberty from the Army program for deporting and detaining these citizens of Japanese extraction. But a judicial construction of the due process clause that will sustain this order is a far more subtle blow to liberty than the promulgation of the order itself. A military order, however unconstitutional, is not apt to last longer than the military emergency. Even during that period a succeeding commander may revoke it all. But once a judicial opinion rationalizes such an order to show that it conforms to the Constitution, or rather rationalizes the Constitution to show that the Constitution sanctions such an order, the Court for all time has validated the principle of racial discrimination in criminal procedure and of transplanting American citizens. The principle then lies about like a loaded weapon ready for the hand of any authority that can bring forward a plausible claim of an urgent need. Every repetition imbeds that principle more deeply in our law and thinking and expands it to new purposes. All who observe the work of courts are familiar with what Judge Cardozo described as

"the tendency of a principle to expand itself to the limit of its logic." A military commander may overstep the bounds of constitutionality, and it is an incident. But if we review and approve, that passing incident becomes the doctrine of the Constitution. There it has a generative power of its own, and all that it creates will be in its own image.

Grant that the function of the court, in reviewing war-power decisions made by the military, the President, and Congress, is not to determine whether those decisions were reasonable in the light of all the circumstances down to the date of judicial review—a very questionable concession. Grant further that the function of the court is not to substitute its judgment for that of the military, the President, and Congress on a basis of what it would have regarded as reasonable in the situation obtaining at the time of the military action—though the substantial-basis test to some degree requires just that. Grant, finally, that even with respect to military orders not strictly military in character that affect civilians within the country, the court, reviewing the military as it would a civilian agency making the same decision, must allow a fair amount of latitude to the military both in deciding whether and to what extent a danger exists and in choosing the means to cope with it. Grant all this, and the role of the court in the Japanese American episode of World War II was still one of the great failures in its history. . . .

In terms of procedure and substance—rather than of the deprivation of constitutional rights which the high judges condoned—the failure of the Supreme Court consisted in:

1. Its failure to apply the substantial-basis test to the question of whether the discriminatory curfew for Japanese American citizens was reasonably necessary and appropriate as a means of preventing espionage and sabotage in the circumstances.

2. Its refusal to pass upon and hold unconstitutional the program of detention.

3. That, with respect to evacuation, it either abandoned the Constitution to military fiat or, what amounts to the same thing, applied the substantial-basis test in such a way as to leave the test meaningless.

4. That it attributed to the military a conclusion that the war crisis justified evacuation at the time it was ordered,

without requiring (*a*) evidence that this was in fact the judgment of the military and (*b*) evidence that the conclusion was reasonably founded.

5. That it sustained the discriminatory evacuation of Japanese Americans, aliens and citizens, without requiring the military to supply substantial evidence (*a*) that there was danger of sabotage and espionage from the group, (*b*) that such danger was not already detected and controlled by existing methods, including curfew, (*c*) that the disloyal could not be separated from the loyal by other and less drastic methods than evacuation within the time limits.

6. That it apparently failed to realize and certainly failed to hold that a decision might be based on grounds so untenable and ridiculous—as that racial strains are determinants of national loyalty—that not only folly but bad motive is proved thereby, and the decision is thus constitutionally void as discriminatory in its purpose.

7. That it gave the most perfunctory scrutiny to a ruinously harsh discrimination based on race and ancestry which in moral terms deserves, and in constitutional terms requires, the most rigid scrutiny; and by this default the United States Supreme Court elevated racism to a constitutional principle.

In this way did the United States Supreme Court strike a blow at the liberties of us all.

4

Balancing Freedom and National Security: A Response to Criticism of the Supreme Court Internment Decisions

William H. Rehnquist

William H. Rehnquist was appointed chief justice of the United States in 1986; he had previously served as a Supreme Court associate justice since 1972. He has written several books on legal history including *The Supreme Court: A History* and *All the Laws but One: Civil Liberties in Wartime*, from which the following passage is excerpted.

Rehnquist examines three Supreme Court decisions—*Hirabayashi v. United States*, *Korematsu v. United States*, and *Endo v. United States*—that generally upheld the constitutionality of the government's removal of Japanese Americans from the West Coast. Some historians and observers have criticized these decisions for failing to protect the civil liberties of Japanese Americans, for deferring too much to military judgment, and for being based on racial distinctions. Rehnquist contends that some of these criticisms are justified, but some are not. He argues that more distinctions should have been made between first-generation Japanese immigrants (the Issei), who were not American citizens, and their American-born children (the Nisei), who were, and that merely restricting access to sensitive military zones would have been more justifiable than relocation and mass detention. But he also argues that the military needed to make prompt decisions in the wake of Pearl Harbor to protect American vulnerabilities to attack and sabotage, and the Supreme Court acted reasonably in not overturning the military's actions.

The judgment of postwar public opinion was that the forced relocation and detention of people of Japanese ancestry was a grave injustice to the great majority who were loyal to the United States. Eugene Rostow, then a professor at Yale Law School and later its dean, writing in 1945, declared the program "a disaster." He criticized it as representing an abandonment of our traditional subordination of military to civil authority, and as sanctioning racially based discrimination against those of Japanese ancestry. Edward Ennis, who as a lawyer in the Justice Department had opposed the adoption of the program, reappeared nearly forty years later on behalf of the American Civil Liberties Union to testify before the congressionally created commission investigating this wartime episode. He characterized the program as "the worst blow to civil liberty in our history."

In the view of the present author, some of this criticism is well justified, and some not; its principal fault is that it lumps together the cases of the Issei—immigrants from Japan—and the Nisei—children of those immigrants who were born in the United States and citizens of the United States by reason of that fact.

The cases before the Supreme Court—*Hirabayashi* [v. *United States*], *Korematsu* [v. *United States*], and *Endo* [v. *United States*]—all involved Nisei. The basis on which the Court upheld the plan was military representations as to the necessity for evacuation. These representations were undoubtedly exaggerated, and they were based in part on the view that not only the Issei but the Nisei were different from other residents of the west coast.

The Military's Role

In defense of the military, it should be pointed out that these officials were not entrusted with the protection of anyone's civil liberties; their task instead was to make sure that vital areas were as secure as possible from espionage or sabotage. The role of General (John L.) DeWitt, the commander of the west coast military department, was not one to encourage a nice calculation of the costs in civil liberties as opposed to the benefits to national security. Contributing to this attitude would have been the news that General Walter Short, the army commander in Hawaii, and Admiral Husband E. Kimmel, the navy commander there, were both summarily removed from their commands ten days after Pearl Harbor because of their failure to anticipate the Japanese surprise attack. DeWitt was surely going to err on the side of caution in making his calculations. . . .

The United States prides itself on a system in which the civilian heads of the service departments are supreme over the military chiefs, so one might expect that [Secretary of War] Henry Stimson and [Assistant Secretary of War] John McCloy would have made a more careful evaluation of the evacuation proposal than they appear to have done. Far from the west coast, they would be expected to have a more detached view than the commander on the scene. But here too there seems to have been a tendency to feel that concern for civil liberties was not their responsibility. There is even more of this feeling in Roosevelt's perfunctory approval of the plan in response to a telephone call from Stimson. [Attorney General Francis] Biddle's protests proved to be futile even at the highest levels of government, in part because no significant element of public opinion opposed the relocation. The American Civil Liberties Union, for example, which filed briefs in the Supreme Court supporting both *Hirabayashi* and *Korematsu* when those cases were argued, was noticeably silent at the time that the program was put into operation.

Questions Facing the Supreme Court

Once the relocation plan was in place, it could only be challenged in the courts. Was the Supreme Court at fault in upholding first the curfew, in *Hirabayashi*, and then the relocation in *Korematsu*? In *Hirabayashi*, the first case, the Court could have decided the validity of both the relocation requirement and the curfew requirement. The "concurrent sentence" doctrine under which the Court declined to do so is not mandatory but discretionary. But counseling against any broader decision was the well-established rule that the Court should avoid deciding constitutional questions if it is possible to do so. Both the curfew and the relocation program were challenged on constitutional grounds, but the latter was a much more serious infringement of civil liberty than the former. The *Hirabayashi* decision, upholding only the curfew, left the more difficult question of the relocation program for another day.

In defense of the military, it should be pointed out that these officials were not entrusted with the protection of anyone's civil liberties.

When that day came—as it did in *Korematsu*—a majority of the Court upheld the relocation program. Justice [Hugo] Black's opinion for the Court in *Korematsu* followed the same line of reasoning as had Chief Justice [Harlan F.] Stone's in *Hirabayashi*. But this time there were three dissenters; they had voted to uphold the curfew but voted to strike down the relocation program.

Several criticisms of the Court's opinions in these cases have been made. The most general is of its extremely deferential treatment of the government's argument that the curfew and relocation were necessitated by military considerations. Here one can only echo Justice [Robert H.] Jackson's observation in his dissenting opinion that "in the very nature of things, military decisions are not susceptible of intelligent judicial appraisal." But it surely does not follow from this that a court must therefore invalidate measures based on military judgments. Eugene Rostow suggests the possibility of a judicial inquiry into the entire question of military necessity, but this seems an extraordinarily dubious proposition. Judicial inquiry, with its restrictive rules of evidence, orientation towards resolution of factual disputes in individual cases, and long delays, is ill-suited to determine an issue such as "military necessity." The necessity for prompt action was cogently stated by the Court in its *Hirabayashi* opinion:

> Although the results of the attack on Pearl Harbor were not fully disclosed until much later, it was known that the damage was extensive, and that the Japanese by their successes had gained a naval superiority over our forces in the Pacific which might enable them to seize Pearl Harbor, our largest naval base and the last stronghold of defense lying between Japan and the West Coast. That reasonably prudent men charged with the responsibility of our national defense had ample ground for conclud-

ing that they must face the danger of invasion, take measures against it, and in making the choice of measures consider our internal situation, cannot be doubted.

Racial Distinctions

A second criticism is that the decisions in these cases upheld a program that, at bottom, was based on racial distinctions. There are several levels at which this criticism can be made. The broadest is that the Nisei were relocated simply because the Caucasian majority on the west coast (and in the country as a whole) disliked them and wished to remove them as neighbors or as business competitors. The Court's answer to this broad attack seems satisfactory—those of Japanese descent were displaced because of fear that disloyal elements among them would aid Japan in the war. Though there were undoubtedly nativists in California who welcomed a chance to see the Issei and the Nisei removed, it does not follow that this point of view was attributable to the military decisionmakers. They, after all, did not at first propose relocation.

Judicial inquiry . . . is ill-suited to determine an issue such as "military necessity."

But a narrower criticism along the same line has more force to it: the Nisei were evacuated notwithstanding the fact that they were American citizens, and they were treated differently from other Americans. Even in wartime, citizens may not be rounded up and required to prove their loyalty. They may be excluded from sensitive military areas in the absence of a security clearance and may otherwise be denied access to any classified information. But it pushes these propositions to an extreme to say that a sizable geographical area, including the residences of many citizens, may be declared off-limits and the residents required to move. It pushes it to an even greater extreme to say that such persons may be required not only to leave their homes but also to report to and remain in a distant relocation center.

The Supreme Court in its *Hirabayashi* opinion pointed to several facts thought to justify this treatment of the Nisei. Both federal and state restrictions on the rights of Japanese emigrants had prevented their assimilation into the Caucasian population and had intensified their insularity and solidarity. Japanese parents sent their children to Japanese-language schools outside of regular school hours, and there was some evidence that the language schools were a source of Japanese nationalistic propaganda. As many as ten thousand American-born children of Japanese parentage went to Japan for all or part of their education. And even though children born in the United States of Japanese alien parents were U.S. citizens, they were under Japanese law also viewed as citizens of Japan. The Court therefore concluded:

> Whatever views we may entertain regarding the loyalty to this country of the citizens of Japanese ancestry, we cannot reject as unfounded the judgment of the military authorities and of Congress that there were disloyal members of that population, whose number and strength could not be precisely and quickly ascertained. We cannot say that the war-making branches of the Government did not have ground for believing that in a critical hour such persons could not readily be isolated and separately dealt with, and constituted a menace to the national defense and safety, which demanded that prompt and adequate measures be taken to guard against it.

There is considerable irony, of course, in relying on previously existing laws discriminating against Japanese immigrants to conclude that still further disabilities should be imposed upon them because they had not been assimilated into the Caucasian majority. But in time of war a nation may be required to respond to a condition without making a careful inquiry as to how that condition came about. . . .

Fears of Invasion

The discrimination against the Nisei lay in the fact that any other citizen could remain in his home unless actually tried and convicted of espionage or sabotage, while the Nisei were removed from their homes without any individualized findings at all. The proffered justification was that attack on or invasion of the west coast by Japan was reasonably feared, and that first-generation American citizens of Japanese descent were more likely than the citizenry as a whole to include potential spies or saboteurs who would assist the enemy.

This view was not totally without support. A "Magic intercept," resulting from the Americans having broken the

Japanese code, dated May 1941, contained a message from the Japanese consulate in Los Angeles that "we also have connections with our second-generations working in airplane plants for intelligence purposes." Such information might well have justified exclusion of Nisei, as opposed to other citizens, from work in aircraft factories without strict security clearance, but it falls considerably short of justifying the dislodging of thousands of citizens from their homes on the basis of ancestry. The submissions by the military showed no particular factual inquiry into the likelihood of espionage or sabotage by Nisei, only generalized conclusions that they were "different" from other Americans. But the military has no special expertise in this field, and it should have taken far more substantial findings to justify this sort of discrimination, even in wartime.

Japanese Aliens

The Issei, however, who were not citizens, were both by tradition and by law in a quite different category. The legal difference dates back to the Alien Law enacted in 1798, during the administration of President John Adams. Often bracketed together with the Sedition Act passed at the same time, there is a tendency to think that both were repealed as soon as Thomas Jefferson and his Jeffersonian Republicans came to power in 1801. But while the Sedition Act expired under its own terms, the Alien Act, with minor amendments, remained on the books at the time of World War II. It provided:

> Whenever there is a declared war between the United States and any foreign nation or government . . . all natives, citizens, denizens, or subjects of the hostile nation or government, being of the age of fourteen years and upward, who shall be within the United States and not actually naturalized, shall be liable to be apprehended, restrained, secured, and removed as alien enemies. The President is authorized, in any such event, by his proclamation thereof . . . to direct the conduct to be observed, on the part of the United States, toward the aliens who become so liable; the manner and degree of the restraint to which they shall be subjected and in what cases, and upon what security their residence shall be permitted, and to provide for the removal of those who, not being permitted to reside within the United States, refuse or neglect to depart therefrom.

In a case decided shortly after the end of World War II, the Supreme Court, referring to the Alien Law, said:

> Executive power over enemy aliens, undelayed and un-hampered by litigation, has been deemed, throughout our history, essential to war-time security. This is in keeping with the practice of the most enlightened of nations and has resulted in treatment of alien enemies more considerate than that which has prevailed among any of our enemies and some of our allies. This statute was enacted or suffered to continue by men who helped found the Republic and formulate the Bill of Rights, and although it obviously denies enemy aliens the con-stitutional immunities of citizens, it seems not then to have been supposed that a nation's obligations to its foes could ever be put on a parity with those of its de-fenders.
>
> The resident enemy alien is constitutionally sub-ject to summary arrest, internment and deportation whenever a "declared war" exists.

Distinctions that might not be permissible between classes of citizens must be viewed otherwise when drawn between classes of aliens.

Thus, distinctions that might not be permissible between classes of citizens must be viewed otherwise when drawn be-tween classes of aliens.

German and Italian Nationals

The most frequently made charge on behalf of the Issei is that the government treated Japanese enemy aliens differ-ently from enemy aliens of German or Italian citizenship, when we were at war with all three countries. It appears that there was some removal of Italian enemy aliens along the west coast for a brief period of time. But there seems little doubt that the west coast Issei were treated quite differently from the majority of German or Italian nationals residing in this country. It should be pointed out, however, that there do not appear to have been the same concentrations of German or Italian nationals along the west coast in areas near major defense plants. Japanese emigration to the United States had occurred entirely within the preceding half-century, and the emigrants resided almost entirely on the west coast; Italian emigration had taken place over a considerably longer period of time, and German emigration had gone on since colonial days. People of German and Italian ancestry were far more spread out in the population in general than were the Issei. While there were areas of German or Italian concentration on the eastern seaboard, the danger feared there was not attacks from German bombers or invasion of German troops, but the sinking of Allied merchant ships by German submarines.

There was the very real fear of attack by Japanese bombers . . . if not actual invasion by Japanese ground forces.

On the west coast, on the other hand, there was the very real fear of attack by Japanese bombers flying from aircraft carriers, if not actual invasion by Japanese ground forces. As noted before, these fears were all but groundless after the Battle of Midway in June 1942, but the relocation program was established and put into effect before that decisive encounter. And as Chief Justice Stone pointed out in *Hirabayashi*, United States aircraft production was highly concentrated on the west coast. The capacity of those plants might have been greatly reduced by a successful air raid, and there is some evidence that residents of Japanese ancestry, loyal to Japan, had been placed in the aircraft plants.

These distinctions seem insufficient to justify such a sharp difference of treatment between Japanese and German and Italian aliens in peacetime. But they do seem legally adequate to support the difference in treatment between the two classes of enemy aliens in time of war.

Chapter 3

Legacies and Lingering Disputes Concerning the Internment of Japanese Americans

1

Internment Centers for Japanese Americans Should Be Called Concentration Camps

James Hirabayashi

In many museum exhibits, historical markers, and historical literature, the internment centers that housed Japanese Americans during World War II are labeled as "concentration camps." Some people have objected to this term, arguing that it inaccurately equates the internment camps with the Nazi concentration camps in which millions of Jews and others were tortured and methodically killed. In the following selection, anthropologist James Hirabayashi argues that the internment centers were, by definition, concentration camps, and that calling them anything else—such as "relocation centers"—would be a way of covering up a shameful historical episode through euphemistic language. The U.S. government deliberately used such language ("evacuation" for forced removal, "non-alien" for citizen) in the course of implementing its policy toward Japanese Americans, he contends.

It was almost 20 years ago when I read an article by Dexter Waugh in the *San Francisco Examiner* titled "Semantic debates on war camps" (May 7, 1976). The issue revolved around the use of terminology on a plaque commemorating Tule Lake as a state historical landmark. At that time I exchanged several letters with the chair of the State Historical

From "Concentration Camp or Relocation Center: What's in a Name?" by James Hirabayashi, *Japanese American National Museum Quarterly*, vol. 9, no. 3 (Fall 1994). Reprinted by permission of the publisher.

Resources Commission, a fellow anthropologist, who voted against the use of the term "concentration camp," saying that he did not believe in editorializing on these plaques. I argued that we should call them what Webster calls them: "places where political prisoners are placed under armed guards." Furthermore, to use "relocation center" was actually editorializing as it is a euphemism used by those government officials who had stripped the Japanese Americans of their basic constitutional rights. The debate had begun in 1973, when Manzanar was established as a state historical site, in arguments before the State Historical Resources Commission. The late Edison Uno, as a spokesperson for the Japanese American Citizens League, appeared to state our case. Although the Commission voted against the plea of the Japanese Americans at these hearings, the State Director of Parks and Recreation overruled the Commission and the term "concentration camps" appears on both plaques.

In 1981, Raymond Okamura submitted a comprehensive essay on the subject to the Commission on Wartime Relocation and Internment of Civilians in Seattle. It was subsequently published as "The American Concentration Camps: A Cover-Up Through Euphemistic Terminology" (*The Journal of Ethnic Studies* 10:3, 1982). Terminological usage continued to be discussed in subsequent actions related to the incarceration of the Japanese Americans such as the annual pilgrimages, the repeal of Executive Order 9066, the Redress Movement and the coram nobis court cases (Fred Korematsu, Gordon Hirabayashi, Minoru Yasui). In view of the discussion over the years, it seems strange that we are still debating the use of terms describing this event.

Points of Debate

Let us review the main points of the debate. Over 120,000 residents of the U.S.A., two thirds of whom were American citizens, were incarcerated under armed guard. There were no crimes committed, no trials, and no convictions: the Japanese Americans were political prisoners. To detain American citizens in a site under armed guard surely constitutes a "concentration camp." But what were the terms used by the government officials who were involved in the process and who had to justify these actions? Raymond Okamura provides us with a detailed list of terms. Let's consider three such euphemisms: "evacuation," "relocations,"

Japanese-American families await their departure to an internment center in Santa Anita, California.

and "non-aliens." Earthquake and flood victims are evacuated and relocated. The words refer to moving people in order to rescue and protect them from danger.

To detain American citizens in a site under armed guard surely constitutes a "concentration camp."

The official government policy makers consistently used "evacuation" to refer to the forced removal of the Japanese Americans and the sites were called "relocation centers." These are euphemisms (Webster: "the substitution of an inoffensive terms for one considered offensively explicit") as the terms do not imply forced removal nor incarceration in enclosures patrolled by armed guards. The masking was intentional. Perhaps the most obvious circumlocution was the use of the term "non-alien." This phrase appeared on yellow notice sheets affixed to telephone poles announcing the removal orders: "Pursuant to the provisions of Civilian Exclusion Order No. 92, this Headquarters, dated May 23, 1942, all persons of Japanese ancestry, both aliens and non-alien, will be evacuated from the above area by 12 o'clock noon, P.W.T., Saturday, May 30, 1942."

The Objectives of Euphemistic Language

Exactly what does "non-alien" mean? To whom does it refer? Of course, it is a euphemism for citizen! Since they were nullifying the constitutional rights of Japanese Americans, it is clear why the government officials did not want to use the term citizen. According to Okamura, euphemistic language accomplished a number of objectives for using the terms: (1) it sidetracked legal and constitutional challenges; (2) it allowed the government to maintain a decent public image; (3) it helped lead the victims into willing cooperation; (4) it permitted the White civilian employees to work without self-reproach; and (5) it kept the historical record in the government's favor. In spite of the official use of the euphemism "relocation center," however, many government officials actually used the term concentration camp including President Franklin D. Roosevelt, General Dwight D. Eisenhower, Secretary of the Interior Harold Ickes, Attorney General Francis Biddle and Supreme Court Justices Owen Robert, Hugo Black and Tom Clark.

The harm in continuing to use the government's euphemisms is that it disguises or softens the reality which subsequently has been legally recognized as a grave error. The action abrogated some fundamental principles underlying the Constitution, the very document under which we govern ourselves. This erosion of fundamental rights has consequences for all citizens of our society and we must see that it is never repeated.

2

Internment Centers for Japanese Americans Should Not Be Called Concentration Camps

Richard Estrada

Richard Estrada was a columnist and associate editor of the *Dallas Morning News*. He argues in the following selection that while the internment of Japanese Americans during World War II was a sad episode in U.S. history, politically motivated historians and activists are distorting the record to make it appear worse than it really was. He especially objects to using the term "concentration camps" to refer to internment camps or relocation centers. Such a term, which inevitably brings to mind Nazi concentration camps, is not a true reflection of how Japanese Americans were treated (there were no gas chambers, for instance), nor does it acknowledge that the U.S. government had legitimate security concerns about aliens of Japanese descent during World War II.

I was walking in Georgetown the other day when a friend from Dallas told me her school-age daughter was being taught about America's "concentration camps" during the Second World War.

Right away I knew what she meant. The painful and complicated issue of how the government treated U.S. residents of Japanese descent was reverberating again, this time during a Sunday stroll up Pennsylvania Avenue.

From "Don't Rewrite Our World War II History," by Richard Estrada, *Dallas Morning News*, September 20, 1996. Reprinted by permission of the *Dallas Morning News*.

A Sad Episode

Everyone agrees it was a sad episode. But more than 50 years since the war's end, the story of the relocation or internment of 125,000 Japanese and Japanese Americans between 1942 and 1946 is getting sadder all the time. Sadder because politically motivated historical revisionists are distorting the facts to the detriment of America.

Exercising the politics of aggrievement, Japanese American advocates and their politically correct allies have already succeeded in getting the state of California to erect a historical marker mistakenly designating the first of the relocation camps as a concentration camp. Now they are trying to get the U.S. government to describe the camp at Manzanar, Calif., as an internment camp, which it was not. . . .

What's in a name? The term "concentration camp" has carried evil connotations since it was first used by Spanish military officials against Cuban rebels in the late 19th century. But it became truly synonymous with inhumanity when the Nazis used concentration camps to stage the Holocaust in Europe.

As for the difference between relocation camps and internment camps, the latter were in fact reserved for persons of Japanese, German and Italian descent disloyal to the United States or prepared to help its wartime enemies. There was a world of difference between persons removed from the West Coast to relocation camps because their loyalty simply was not known and persons known to be loyal to the Axis powers who were sent to internment camps. Since World War II, declassified and decoded Japanese intelligence messages intercepted by the United States during the war have proved that the government did have knowledge of Fifth Column activity.

Whether at U.S. relocation camps or authentic internment camps, there were no gas chambers and no killing fields. Children were not separated from parents, nor husbands from wives and children. As one former Manzanar resident, who was a teen-ager at the time, told a Japanese American newspaper in 1994, "we got three square meals a day and could play all day long."

Politically Motivated History

Politically motivated revisionism deflects attention from genuinely unjust policies. For Congress to have passed laws in the 19th century that persons of Asian descent could be barred admission or denied citizenship, was a racist conceit whose demise was contained in its own rotten core. But once the United States found itself at war with Japan, there was no viable option but to designate noncitizens of Japanese, German and Italian heritage as "enemy aliens."

The attempt to portray events as worse than they were is morally indefensible. And not only because it unfairly casts aspersions on good and decent people faced with enormous leadership responsibilities at a moment of national crisis. It sabotages our sense of national unity and purpose by spawning distrust among the nation's ethnic groups.

The attempt to portray events as worse than they were is morally indefensible.

It is neither offensive nor mean-spirited to assert that persons of Japanese origin did not suffer anywhere near as much as European Jews. Nor is it an affront to Japanese Americans to note that they were not singled out on the basis of ethnicity, but rather on the question of their alienage, noncitizenship, dual citizenship and, in some instances, their refusal to swear allegiance to the United States during wartime. The racism argument was rejected in the Supreme Court's Korematsu decision of 1944, which still stands. Legislation passed in 1987 to compensate such individuals for "human suffering" was, in contrast, a political decision.

A Slander Against the United States

Every American has a responsibility to protest the mistreatment of individuals or groups. And it must be emphasized that great loyalty was demonstrated by many Japanese Americans and noncitizens in spite of the disloyalty of others.

But U.S. citizens have a responsibility to challenge an injustice against the American people as a whole. That is precisely what the racially aggrieved or the politically correct are perpetrating when they promote the slander that the United States ran concentration camps during World War II, or that no evidence was available to the government to support fears of subversive activity on the West Coast.

The rewriting of history to support a political position has perpetuated ethnic conflicts worldwide. That should be reason enough for Americans to insist on the truth.

3

The Japanese-American Community and the Struggle for Redress

Gary Y. Okihiro

Historian Gary Y. Okihiro describes the political activism of Japanese Americans and its effects on the Japanese-American community in the years following World War II. Many Japanese Americans at first internalized their wartime experiences and did not speak out about them. However, beginning in the 1960s, some Japanese Americans, including children and grandchildren of those interned, began to seek redress and reparations from the U.S. government. Okihiro writes that their activities, while initially controversial among some elements of the Japanese-American community, eventually served to mobilize that community and encourage victims of internment to break their silence about the camps, to confront painful memories, and to demand appropriate redress. Their efforts were rewarded when Congress passed the Civil Rights Act of 1988, which included a formal apology from Congress and financial redress of $20,000 for surviving victims of internment. Gary Y. Okihiro is a professor of history and director of the Asian American studies program at Cornell University in New York.

A lthough a small minority, Japanese Americans sought to undo the restrictions of the past and help shape their future by engaging in the political process. A pivotal moment was the passage of the Immigration and Nationality Act of 1952, which removed race as a criterion for naturalization

Excerpted from *Whispered Silences: Japanese Americans and World War II*, by Gary Y. Okihiro. Copyright © 1996 by The University of Washington Press. Reprinted with permission from The University of Washington Press.

but also introduced a quota system that discriminated against Asian immigration and broadened the grounds for the exclusion and deportation of aliens. But the act, passed during the cold war and over the veto of President Harry Truman, enabled citizenship for the *issei*, the vast majority of whom had been rendered perpetual aliens by U.S. law since 1790.". . .

Japanese Americans sought to undo the restrictions of the past and help shape their future by engaging in the political process.

Another law enacted during the cold war and passed over the veto of President Truman, the Internal Security Act of 1950, held significance for Japanese Americans. Title II of the act authorized the president to apprehend and detain any person of whom there was "reasonable ground to believe that such person probably will engage in, probably will conspire with others to engage in, acts of espionage or of sabotage." The precedents established by the U.S. Supreme Court in its decisions affirming the constitutionality of the World War II Japanese American detention program, proponents argued, provided ample authority for the government's sweeping powers during national emergencies. Between 1952 and 1958, Congress appropriated funds to prepare and administer six sites, including the Tule Lake concentration camp used for Japanese Americans during World War II, in the event of an emergency. Ten years later, during protests against the Vietnam War and rising Black militancy, Edwin E. Willis, chairman of the House Un-American Activities Committee, favored the use of Title II and declared that "black militants have essentially declared war on the United States, and therefore they lose all constitutional rights and should be imprisoned in detention camps." And in 1969, Deputy Attorney General Richard Kleindienst said of student protesters, "If people demonstrated in a manner to interfere with others, they should be rounded up and put in a detention camp.". . .

Fighting the Internal Security Act

It was Japanese Americans who spearheaded the drive to repeal Title II. In June 1968, Raymond Okamura and Mary Anna Takagi began a grass-roots campaign within the

Japanese American Citizens League (JACL), a *nisei* patriotic and civic organization begun in 1930, to repeal Title II. According to Okamura, the group believed that Japanese Americans, "as the past victims of American concentration camps, were in the best position to lead a repeal campaign," and "it was imperative for Japanese Americans to assume the leadership in order to promote Third World unity. Japanese Americans had been the passive beneficiaries of the Black civil rights movement," he explained, "and this campaign was the perfect issue by which Japanese Americans could make a contribution to the overall struggle for justice in the United States."

The group convinced the conservative JACL leadership to endorse the campaign, and at its national convention in 1968, the JACL adopted a resolution calling for the repeal of Title II. The effort was joined by Hawaii's *nisei* members of Congress in 1969, when [Daniel K.] Inouye and [Spork M.] Matsunaga introduced repeal bills in the Senate and House respectively. As it turned out, the initiative led by Japanese Americans, "the first group in the United States to have concentration camp experience," according to the *Nation* in a June 9, 1969, editorial, disarmed Title II supporters, who had come to view their opposition as "Negro militants" and "alleged radicals" whose motives might be suspect. In 1971, Congress overwhelmingly approved repeal, and President Richard M. Nixon, on his way to a historic meeting with Japan's emperor Hirohito, stopped in Portland, Oregon, to sign the repeal measure.

For over a quarter century the unspeakable crime was quietly internalized by the victims.

Edison Uno, one of the co-chairs of the JACL repeal campaign, reflected upon the meaning of the effort for Japanese Americans. Likening the unconstitutional forced removal and detention of Japanese Americans to rape, Uno wrote [in a 1974 *Amerasia Journal* article]: "For over a quarter century the unspeakable crime was quietly internalized by the victims as they suffered in silence from a false sense of guilt and shame and thought of themselves as American citizens unworthy of their birthright. Their unjust imprisonment, which mocked the American tradition that 'one is considered innocent until proven guilty' created long-lasting psychological problems. The trauma was so great that many believed that they must 'prove' themselves innocent in order to eliminate the preconceived notion that Japanese Americans were categorically disloyal. For the record," he added, "it is well established that not one incident of sabotage or espionage was ever committed by a Japanese American." The repeal campaign that brought together scores of Japanese Americans in a common effort, wrote Uno, indicated a healthy response to the people's trauma, showing that "we realized that we should no longer suffer the pain and agony of false guilt" and instead discovered that "we were truly victims of a conspiracy of officials in government who abused their authority and power in order to victimize helpless citizens." In that way, the campaign to repeal Title II was a coming to terms with the silence imposed by the wartime years and a reminder of the need for constant vigilance in the defense of freedom. "The thrill of victory," foresaw Uno, "must be used to energize the next struggle."

The Redress Movement

Perhaps what Uno had in mind was his 1970 proposal to JACL for that body to seek legislative reparations for the wartime detention. In fact, others before him, such as James Omura, Joseph Y. Kurihara, and Kiyoshi Okamoto, had argued during the war for governmental redress for the wrongs committed and the losses suffered. But it was Edison Uno who prepared the way for the campaign that would culminate with the passage and signing of the Civil Rights Acts of 1988. Uno contended that monetary payments to the victims of the camps would help to ease their economic hardships and mental anguish, vindicate the loyalty of all Japanese Americans, rebuild their shattered communities, educate the American public about the loss of civil liberties, and ensure that such acts never happen again in the future." Although the JACL passed resolutions supporting redress as early as 1970, very little effort was expended on implementing the project until 1976, when it created the National Committee for Redress, which directed JACL's legislative strategy.

The JACL, however, was not the sole actor in the redress movement. The *sansei*, the third generation, were coming of age; and weaned on the social activism of the 1960s, many were inspired by and participants in the civil rights, free speech, anti-Vietnam War and Third World solidarity, women's, and ethnic studies movements. In 1969, the Organization of Southland Asian American Organizations arranged the first pilgrimage to Manzanar concentration camp, students in northern California organized a counterpart pilgrimage to Tule Lake in the same year, and beginning in 1978 activists held Days of Remembrance in communities and on college campuses to commemorate the February 19, 1942, signing of Executive Order 9066. Several hundred people, of all generations, boarded buses to the campsites, cleaned the graves, and remembered the years of exile. "I came on this pilgrimage out of curiosity, little realizing the impact this trip was to have on me," said Marie Miyashiro. "Many feelings which were repressed, many of my 'mental blocks' were cleansed and washed away as I stood on the ground of our former campsite. Realization that I was here once, that I had lost my father in Tule Lake hit me with such a force. I could not stop my flow of tears. More tears flowed later, but these were all good 'cleansing tears.' I feel good. I'm glad reconciliation has taken place with me."

Vindication from the Courts

Another part of that reconciliation was winning vindication from the courts, the very courts that had affirmed the injustice of the mass removal and detention. Peter Irons, a member of the legal studies faculty at the University of Massachusetts at the time, discovered in 1981 that the government's own lawyers arguing the internment cases before the U.S. Supreme Court in 1943 and 1944 complained that their superiors had lied to and suppressed evidence from the court. That finding, Irons told the original litigants, Gordon Hirabayashi, Minoru Yasui, and Fred Korematsu, might make it possible to reopen the cases and clear their criminal convictions. "They did me a great wrong," said Korematsu simply, and so began the effort to right "a great wrong." The team of attorneys pursuing the petitions for a writ of error coram nobis (a rehearing to correct a fundamental error at the original trial) was headed by Irons, Kathryn Bannai, Dale Minami, and Peggy Nagai.

Between 1983 when the first petition was filed and 1988 when the government decided to end the litigation, Fred

Korematsu and Gordon Hirabayashi's wartime convictions were vacated, but the judge refused to hear Minoru Yasui's petition, and the government's decision to drop the matter prevented a full hearing by the Supreme Court, which was the only body capable of reversing its decisions. Still, the effort to right a great wrong was a pivotal moment in the unfinished business of the war. "It is now conceded by almost everyone that the internment of Japanese Americans during World War II was simply a tragic mistake for which American society as a whole must accept responsibility," declared Judge Donald S. Voorhees, who heard the Hirabayashi coram nobis petition. "If in the future, this country should find itself in a comparable national emergency, the sacrifices made by Gordon Hirabayash, Fred Korematsu, and Minoru Yasui may, it is hoped, stay the hand of a government again tempted to imprison a defenseless minority without trial and for no offense."

Meanwhile, the legislative effort for redress continued. In 1976, President Gerald R. Ford, in a symbolic act, repealed Executive Order 9066, and in 1980, largely as a result of a compromise reached by the JACL with the Japanese American members of Congress, a Commission on Wartime Relocation and Internment of Civilians was created by President Jimmy Carter and Congress to ascertain whether an injustice had been committed and to recommend appropriate remedies. The commission was seen by strategists as a necessary intermediate step toward the goal of legislative redress. Groups like the National Council for Japanese American Redress (NCJAR), formed in 1979, and the National Coalition for Redress/Reparations (NCRR), organized in 1980, opposed the commission plan at first, believing that the tactic was simply a way to stall legislative action. NCJAR, led by William Hohri, introduced its own redress bill through Mike Lowry, representative from Washington, but it failed in committee. In 1983, NCJAR filed a class-action lawsuit on behalf of all the victims of the detention camps, and that too eventually failed.

An Outpouring of Testimony

But all of those efforts stirred, then mobilized, a sentiment and movement for redress among a supportive, reluctant, and sometimes antagonistic Japanese American community, some of whom preferred to forget the past. That redress movement, working on different fronts, helped to ensure that the legislative process continued to make progress, and NCRR members lined up and prepared witnesses for the commission's hearings in the summer and fall of 1981, when its nine members solicited testimonies in Washington, D.C., New York City, Chicago, Los Angeles, San Francisco, Seattle, and the Aleutian and Pribilof Islands. Those hearings marked a turning point in the drive for legislative redress by revealing to the government the depth of the people's suffering in the outpouring of their testimonies and by solidifying Japanese American support for the idea of redress. The hearings were a kind of "coming out" for Japanese Americans, who had hidden their shame and guilt, unmerited, in the closets of their minds. With their voices, after nearly forty years, they broke the silences of the camps. . . .

The [redress commission] hearings were a kind of 'coming out' for Japanese Americans, who had hidden their shame . . . in the closets of their minds.

Kanshi Stanley Yamashita told the commissioners that his family was among those evicted from Terminal Island with forty-eight hours' notice. When the eviction order was posted, Yamashita's father had already been picked up by the FBI and sent to the camp at Bismarck, North Dakota. "Without the head of the family, how does a mother, with three children, move out of a house where they have lived for years?" he asked. "Bitter memories of trying to dispose of furniture, a fairly new car, my father's precious sextant and chronometers, and the accumulation of years of living to grubby, calculating and profit-seeking scavengers are still vivid." Yamashita then turned to the charge of the commission: "It is farcical to state that the raison d'être of this Commission is to determine whether a wrong had been committed—rather, its efforts should be directed to rectify the patent wrongs committed against a group, solely on ethnic grounds." After relating some of the skepticism among Japanese Americans about the commission's outcome, Yamashita asked, "What will you members of this Commission do to change the resigned, despairing and fatalistic views of these people who still vividly recall the misery and helpless feelings engendered by the evacuation and have inherited the legacy of bigotry, hatred and racial prejudice?"

"My name is Alice Tanabe Nehira. I was born 5 June 1943 at the Tule Lake Project in Newell, California," she told the commissioners. Her father, Yoriharu Tanabe, was born in Hiroshima, and despite the mass removal order that left many of his friends "angered and betrayed" and the atomic bombing of his place of birth "where most all of his school friends were annihilated," Tanabe, his daughter testified, was "steadfast in his belief that this nation would someday see the grave injustice of this act [detention of Japanese Americans]." When she was born, Nehira continued, the camp physician performed a tubal ligation on her mother without ever telling her or receiving her consent. She discovered her sterility years later when she was examined for colon cancer. "Today, after thirty-eight years, I am still a victim of prejudice," said Nehira, who told about her discrimination suit pending against her employer. "For over thirty-five years I have been the stereotype Japanese American. I've kept quiet, hoping that in due time we will be justly compensated and recognized for our years of patient effort. By my passive attitude, I can reflect on my past years to conclude that it doesn't pay to remain silent. No one benefits when truth is silent." And turning to the commissioners and their work, Nehira declared: "The final judgment will affect all Americans, now and for all time."

"However painful it is, even after forty years of trying to forget the bitter memories of the indignities and hardships suffered by Japanese Americans as a result of the nightmare of the relocation and four years of incarceration, I dedicate this testimony to my children, Ken, Rei, and Kimi, to my brothers Toki and Dick, and to my late father-in-law Gohei Matsuda, and my former mother-in-law Kama, who lived through the frightening experience of wartime internment, in the hope that the tragedy . . . will never again be endured by any American citizen of whatever race or ancestry," began Violet de Cristoforo. A native-born citizen with a seven-year-old son, a five-year-old daughter, and three months pregnant, de Cristoforo and her family were uprooted and placed behind barbed wire. Her daughter was born "in a horse stable" at Fresno Assembly Center and, on the train to Jerome, developed double pneumonia and remained sickly in Jerome and in Tule Lake, where they were transferred. Her brother Toki was placed in Tule Lake's stockade, a prison within a prison, where "he was repeatedly beaten by the security personnel, so badly that once he was left for dead." Her other brother, Dick, served in the U.S. Army in the Pacific as a translator and was called "derogatory names" by his comrades and "made to go into caves in search of documents or interrogate Japanese prisoners, always with some Caucasian members of his unit armed with rifles and bayonets at his back because they did not feel he could be trusted." Her father, who lived in Hiroshima, died and her mother was severely burned as a result of the atomic bomb explosion, de Cristoforo discovered after the war. "I . . . hope," she resolved, "that the authorities will give a solemn pledge that they will remain faithful to the provisions of our constitution and that the indignities and emotional stresses we suffered will not be repeated in the future."

Redress and Compensation

The commission recommended, and Congress passed, the Civil Rights Act of 1988, which contained a formal apology from Congress, presidential pardons for those who resisted the eviction and detention orders, recommendations that government agencies restore to Japanese American employees lost status or entitlements because of the wartime actions, and financial redress to Japanese American individuals and communities, $20,000 to each survivor and the creation of a community fund to educate the American public about the experience. In a reversal of his administration's opposition to redress, President Ronald Reagan signed the bill into law on August 10, 1988, bringing to a close another aspect of the camps' unfinished business.

But the totality of that business will only be completed when we can ensure that the violation will "never again be endured by any American citizen," in de Cristoforo's words, and that assurance—that racism (or sexism or homophobia or nativism) will never again shape and justify government policy and action—can only be given when we the people resolve it.

4

Draft Resistance by Some Internees Has Left Divisions Within the Japanese-American Community

Norihiko Shirouzu

During their wartime internment, young Japanese-American men were faced with a choice of how to respond when the U.S. government sought to enroll them in the U.S. armed forces. The different choices they made divided the camps then and, as journalist Norihiko Shirouzu writes in the following selection, continue to divide the Japanese-American community to this day.

Following Pearl Harbor, many Japanese Americans already in the armed forces were summarily discharged or assigned to noncombat positions. In addition, Japanese Americans not in the armed forces were classified 4-F (unfit for service) by the Selective Service System. Their classification was subsequently changed to 4-C (enemy aliens ineligible for service) even though they were American citizens. However, in 1943, the U.S. Army decided to reclassify Japanese Americans as 1-A (eligible for service) and asked Japanese Americans in Hawaii and in the internment camps to consider volunteering for a segregated unit. In early 1944, the government made the military draft applicable to Japanese Americans in the camps.

Some internees chose military service as a way both to help the war effort and to prove the loyalty of Japanese Americans to the United States; many became part of the highly decorated 442nd Regimental Combat Team. Others refused to enlist or chose to become draft resisters, citing the unfair treatment of Japanese Americans and demanding that the camps be closed. Many were convicted of violating the Selective Service Act and sent to federal prison.

Shirouzu, a staff reporter for the *Wall Street Journal*, describes how these differing choices created animosities within the Japanese-American community that still exist today. Many World War II veterans remain scornful of those who chose draft resistance. Former draft resistors, who initially kept a low profile after the war, have become more critical of Japanese-American leaders (especially the Japanese American Citizens League) for failing to acknowledge the sacrifices they made and the reasons behind them. Efforts to reconcile these warring elements within the Japanese-American community have had mixed success, Shirouzu concludes.

In 1944, as America's war with Japan raged in the Pacific, Mits Koshiyama received his draft orders from Uncle Sam. Then, as now, he considered it his moral obligation not to answer the call. After all, he was languishing behind barbed wire, one of the roughly 110,000 Japanese-Americans imprisoned by the U.S. government as potential subversives.

"How could we have fought for democracy and freedom overseas when we were denied the very same rights by our own government?" Mr. Koshiyama says.

> *To . . . many . . . Japanese-American veterans, the [draft] resisters betrayed their community.*

The logic escapes Teruo Nobori, and mere mention of Mr. Koshiyama's name makes his blood boil. Mr. Nobori, like Mr. Koshiyama, is a nisei—a second-generation Japanese-American. Unlike Mr. Koshiyama, he is a war hero. "Cowardly draft dodgers" is how he describes the more than 300 Japanese-Americans who defied the draft on civil-rights grounds during World War II. To him and many other Japanese-American veterans, the resisters betrayed their community when it most needed to prove its patriotism. "If the Japanese had landed on U.S. soil, who knows?" he says. "They might've shot the other way."

Festering Animosity

Mr. Koshiyama is now 74 years old; Mr. Nobori, 84. The history that divides them may seem ancient to some, but while the war ended 54 years ago, the animosity has only festered over the decades—mostly in silence. More recently, the old passions have been stoked as younger Japanese-Americans have discovered the story of the draft resisters—and concluded that they have been wrongfully shunned for holding to convictions that, by current sensibilities, were justified.

"It was liberating to discover . . . Mr. Koshiyama in our history," says Kenji Taguma, a third-generation Japanese-American who didn't learn of the resisters until undertaking a high-school term paper a decade ago. These men are proof, he says, that "some of our own people had the courage to fight our own government's oppression and racism."

Younger Japanese-Americans have . . . concluded that [draft resisters] have been wrongfully shunned for holding to convictions that, by current sensibilities, were justified.

Few disagree that the root cause of this rift—the imprisonment of Japanese-Americans—is a disgraceful episode in U.S. history. After Japan's attack on Pearl Harbor in 1941, the U.S. government deemed most Japanese-Americans on the West Coast to be potential "subversive enemy elements," evicting them from their homes and businesses, stripping them of their U.S. citizenship, and confining them in prison camps.

The U.S. government acknowledged the mistake much later, in 1988, paving the way for financial reparations to Japanese-Americans for a racially motivated violation of their civil rights. (Whites of German and Italian ancestry weren't systematically incarcerated.)

But how was a young man behind a chain-link fence to act when, in January 1944, the government that had denied his family its civil rights asked him to fight for it? Many answered the call. Some, like Mr. Nobori, volunteered. He fought in the all-nisei 442nd Regimental Combat Team, which gained acclaim by giving 140 lives and suffering 674 wounded to save 211 soldiers isolated behind German lines deep in a French forest in the closing days of the war.

"We were being tested on our loyalty to America. Is that time to resist?" says Mr. Nobori, a retiree from the produce business who lives in Albany, Calif. "If you were American at heart, you wanted to do all you could to make yourself a real American."

Draft Resisters

But a vocal minority rebelled. These men refused induction orders and openly urged compatriots to do the same. They would go to war, they said, only if the government restored their citizenship and released their families.

Frank Emi was a leader of the resisters and inspired hundreds more to buck the draft. "You get uprooted, kicked around, stomped on, and they asked you to fight for the very government who orchestrated all that," says Mr. Emi, now 82 and living in the Los Angeles suburb of San Gabriel. "It was insult to injury."

Many of the resisters were convicted of violating the Selective Service Act and sent to federal prison. Mr. Koshiyama was convicted in 1944 in a mass trial of about 60 resisters in Cheyenne, Wyo., and sent to McNeil Island Federal Penitentiary in Washington state. He was released for good behavior in the summer of 1946, after serving 26 months of his three-year sentence, and returned to his home in San Jose, Calif. Like others, he feels he made his peace with the government after President [Harry] Truman extended a full pardon to the resisters in December 1947.

But he still hasn't made peace with the broader Japanese-American community, and particularly with the Japanese American Citizens League. The JACL, a community group that led the patriotic faction during the war and now has 24,500 members, remains one of the dominant Japanese-American organizations in the country. Its stated purpose: "to fight discrimination against people of Japanese ancestry."

"I'm still upset about the JACL," Mr. Koshiyama says. "They demanded and received an apology from the government, but they haven't faced up to what they did to the community's own dissenters like us."

For Mr. Koshiyama and the others, the ostracism began

in the prison camps and persisted for decades. At Heart Mountain, an internment camp in Wyoming where Mr. Emi was imprisoned, a group called the Fair Play Committee counseled nisei men to ignore the draft. The *Heart Mountain Sentinel*, the official camp newspaper, excoriated Fair Play leaders like Mr. Emi, calling them "wild-eyed," "slow-witted," "warp-minded" rabble-rousers who "lacked physical and moral courage."

George Ishikawa, an 84-year-old resister in Mountain View, Calif., says his wife, Barbara, endured much hostility in the camp and long after the war. After he was arrested at Heart Mountain, she came under continual verbal assault from camp neighbors. He says she was once told that "there's no future for your kids in this country." Mrs. Ishikawa declined to discuss the matter.

Upon release from prison, most resisters returned to the West Coast, but fearing backlash against their families, most kept low profiles in the Japanese-American community. "We were such a minority," Mr. Ishikawa says. "We tried to live quietly, not to be noticed."

The Vietnam War, with its protests and conscientious objectors, brought back the bitterness. Mr. Ishikawa recalls a party in the 1960s at the Buddhist church his family attended in Mountain View. An acquaintance he and his wife had known from childhood stood up, looked directly at the couple, and announced: "Men who resist the draft don't deserve to be in this country."

The JACL's Version of History

Much of the hostility toward the resisters, says Frank Chin, a Chinese-American who has written extensively on the resisters, can be traced to what he calls "myth making" by Japanese-American groups, particularly the JACL. The league, he says, long promoted a version of history in which Japanese-Americans willingly accepted the prison camps as their contribution to America's war effort, and in which nisei soldiers proved the community's unwavering loyalty to the U.S.

True, enthusiasm for the draft was real in Hawaii, where there was no mass internment of Japanese-Americans: About 13,500 volunteered or responded to the draft there, accounting for more than half of the 22,235 Japanese-American men who fought during the war, according to

Roger Daniels, a professor of history at the University of Cincinnati. But on the mainland, only 1,943 of the more than 20,000 eligible Japanese-American men volunteered, while 2,795 answered induction orders, Prof. Daniels says.

Herb Yamanishi, national director of the JACL in San Francisco, says it was "not the JACL's official policy" to bend history to its view, but he acknowledges that certain members may have done so on their own. One of those historians, Bill Hosokawa, says he tried to "present the bright side" of the community in his writings. But he insists that the lack of mention of the resisters in his writings was merely an oversight. "I just didn't think about them," he says.

The resisters, too, played a part in keeping themselves out of history. When Mr. Chin interviewed several resisters and some Fair Play Committee leaders in the early 1980s, most didn't want their names attached to anything he planned to publish. Many resisters also went years without telling their children about their wartime actions.

Now, it is a younger generation of Japanese-Americans who have been forcing open the file on the resisters. Discovering their tale has answered a question that many long asked: Why did 110,000 Japanese-Americans apparently become model prisoners so willingly and meekly? Obviously, not all of them did.

A Son's Discovery

Mr. Taguma discovered the resisters through a high-school project. Now editor of the *Nichi Bei Times*, a Japanese-American daily in San Francisco, he says that uncovering the diversity of the community's response to the war gave him "a tremendous sense of pride" as a Japanese-American.

It also deeply changed his view of his father. When he was growing up, Mr. Taguma, now 29 years old, never got along with his father, Noboru. His father was a "mean guy," often "very irritable" and given to pacing the house, muttering, "You don't know about us guys," and, "You guys don't know anything about suffering." His father had never told him about his past as a draft resister.

Then in 1987, while he was writing a term paper about Japanese-Americans' wartime experience, Mr. Taguma says, his father began telling him about his past. Noboru Taguma says he hadn't hidden his past, but that he only wanted to make sure that his son was "mature enough" to understand the issues involved.

Kenji Taguma says the importance of his father's action didn't dawn on him right away. It had to wait until the fall of 1991, when he took a class in Asian-American studies with lecturer Wayne Maeda, an activist on behalf of the resisters who encouraged him to organize an exhibit on the resistance movement.

Since then, "there has been a tremendous turnaround" in the relationship between father and son, Mr. Taguma says. "I take pride in what my father did," he says. "My father was a resister at a time when it was really unpopular to take a stance like that. His legacy of resistance will always be with me." Mr. Taguma now uses his Western middle name, Glenn, less and his Japanese first name, Kenji, more.

Attempts at Reconciliation

Resolution of that sort eludes the broader Japanese-American community, despite several attempts at reconciliation. In 1999, several nisei veterans groups officially acknowledged that the resisters were acting on just principles. In 1990, the JACL approved a resolution saying that it "regrets any pain and bitterness caused by its failure to recognize this group of patriotic Americans." Critics say that doesn't go far enough.

Several nisei veterans groups officially acknowledged that the resisters were acting on just principles.

In the summer of 1994, the JACL's more liberal members led an effort to investigate the league's role in ignoring the resisters' story and saw an opportunity for the group to offer a public apology. They invited resister leaders like Mr. Emi to Salt Lake City for the league's national convention. But the maneuvering by the league's old guard blocked full debate on the issue, and the resisters went home without an apology.

In 1995, the league district that represents Southern California and Southern Nevada formally apologized to the resisters. Only one district has followed suit since, and the other six districts are still weighing similar resolutions.

Some veterans have softened their stance. Tom Saka-moto, a nisei veteran who once shouted down Mr. Emi and Mr. Chin in a public forum in Oakland, says he has changed his mind on resisters. He says he understands that they were acting in good conscience, and "my heart goes out to them."

But others, like Karl Kinaga, a 75-year-old veteran and longtime Japanese-American community leader in San Jose, continue to consider the resisters traitors. Mr. Kinaga says the resisters who have come out of the closet have grossly misled the Japanese-American public by refusing to address one issue: While some of the 315 resisters "didn't want to get shot at," many others refused the draft because "their fa-thers were pro-Japan," he alleges.

That's an explosive charge among Japanese-Americans, and Mr. Koshiyama, among others, dismisses it as pure speculation. The war government and the JACL would have jumped at the chance to lodge similar accusations against the resisters during the war, Mr. Koshiyama says. "But they couldn't and didn't because they had no basis for claims like that," he says. Nor does anyone today, he adds. Those who make them, he says, "just hate our guts."

5

America's Version of Holocaust Revisionists

Robert Ito

A vocal minority of historians, World War II veterans, and others have argued that the internment of Japanese Americans during World War II was not as bad as many believe and have questioned whether Japanese Americans were truly incarcerated. In the following essay, Robert Ito compares these "revisionists" to those who deny the existence of the Holocaust. He contends that they make selective use of historical evidence in their arguments, which are receiving greater circulation through the Internet. Ito is an assistant editor at *Los Angeles Magazine* and also writes for *Asian Week*.

Since the end of World War II, Holocaust revisionists throughout Europe have vehemently denied that the extermination of 6 million Jews ever took place. The gas chambers? Zionist propaganda. Zyklon B? A heavy duty delousing agent.

But the rewriting of camp history isn't just a European obsession. Over the last two decades, an equally determined band of homegrown revisionists has fought to paint a rosy picture of America's own concentration camps: the ten "relocation centers" where over 120,000 Japanese Americans were imprisoned during World War II.

The debate over the historical interpretation of the American camps was reignited recently by an exhibit at Ellis Island entitled "America's Concentration Camps: Remembering the Japanese American Experience," an exhibit

From "Concentration Camp or Summer Camp?" by Robert Ito, *Mother Jones.com*, September 15, 1998. Reprinted with permission.

that freely uses the term "concentration camp" to describe the isolated encampments at such places as Manzanar and Tule Lake, Calif.; Poston, Ariz.; Topaz, Utah. Critics claim that the use of the term dishonors the victims of the Nazi death camps; supporters argue that the term is historically accurate, and point to the numerous academics, military officials, and even U.S. presidents who have preferred the term over the more euphemistic "internment camp" label.

But while the Japanese American and American Jewish communities bickered over semantics, few sought to downplay the historical and cultural importance of the Japanese American relocation camps: Thousands of American citizens snatched from their homes solely because of their ethnicity, without any evidence of wrongdoing. Whole families placed in barbed-wire encampments under armed guard for years, many losing all of their property in the process. Racial hatred and wartime hysteria justified under the guise of "military necessity" in what former Sen. Sam Ervin described as "the single most blatant violation of the Constitution in our history."

Claims of Revisionists

Some American revisionists, however, see things differently, and they want you to know about it. Among their odder claims:

• Contrary to popular belief, more white people were interned during the war than Japanese Americans (another semantic point: most of the 120,000 Japanese Americans were "relocated," not "interned").

• Most Japanese Americans were never forced into the camps—they received a "government invitation to sit out the war in a Relocation Center."

• Barbed-wire fences around the camps were strung up to "keep out the neighboring farmers' cows" and armed guard towers were used only as lookout sites for dangerous brush fires.

• The camps were so nice that East Coast Japanese Americans unaffected by the West Coast "relocation" were clamoring to get in.

Despite the wackiness of some of their claims, the revisionists are not all talk. Over the last two decades, individuals have threatened to burn down buildings at Manzanar, defaced and fired rounds at a plaque designating the site as a State

Historical Landmark, scrawled swastikas and racials slurs around the area, and even accused Manzanar supporters of treason. And while their numbers are small, their message is reaching ever greater audiences, thanks to the Internet.

Queen of the Revisionists

Until her death in 1996, Lillian Baker reigned supreme as the voice of the internment camp revisionists. A prolific writer, amateur historian, and founder of the International Club for Collectors of Hatpins and Hatpin Holders, Baker fought tenaciously against redress and reparations payments to Japanese American internees and the restoration of the Manzanar camp as a National Historic Site.

According to Sue Kunitomi Embrey, a longtime activist within the redress movement and founder of the Manzanar Committee, Baker was the movement's chief researcher and historian. "She did a lot of research, but she would twist the material to her own advantage," Embrey recalls. "But some things that she would write actually went against what she was going for," Embrey adds. "They revealed what was really happening, although I don't think she realized what she was doing at the time."

[A] determined band of homegrown revisionists has fought to paint a rosy picture of America's own concentration camps.

Baker's beef with the redress movement? Her primary argument was that the camps were a "military necessity," a defense made during the war but later rejected by the national Commission on Wartime Relocation and Internment of Civilians. Baker's followers supported the argument with their own bone-chilling accounts of foreign intrigue— accounts of repeated Japanese Navy attacks on the Oregon coastline, even a "top secret" revelation entitled "Yes, the Japanese Had an Atomic Bomb."

While their stories often contain elements of truth— Oregon was hit by one deadly balloon bomb and a lone Japanese pilot did make an abortive attempt to start forest fires in the Oregon woods—they all tend to make the mistake of lumping together the Japanese military and Japanese American citizens. According to Bill Michael, director of the Inyo County–based Eastern California Museum and frequent combatant with the local historical revisionists because of his museum's Manzanar exhibit, this inability to distinguish between the two groups is fairly common. "Quite often what happens is an intermingling of the Bataan Death March with this issue," Michael says. "They're equating the American citizens in this camp with the Emperor's army, basically."

The Summer Camp Argument

Baker's other argument—graphically illustrated in one of her books by photographs of smiling Japanese American schoolkids placed alongside grim images from the Nazi death camps—was that our "relocation centers," by comparison, really were not all that bad. Baker defended this claim through selective photo editing, with the harsher, more revealing photos of the Japanese American camps ending up on her cutting room floor.

Baker also supported her "summer camp" argument by quoting liberally from a few ultraconservatives within the Japanese American community itself. Republican Sen. S.I. Hayakawa of California, who led the movement to declare English the official language of the U.S. and gained notoriety for his hardball tactics during the San Francisco State student strike, was one of Baker's favorite sources. In one essay, Hayakawa attacked the proponents of the redress movement as "young Japanese-Americans following a fashion established by black militants" and defended the camps as necessary safehouses against rioting white mobs.

> *The Internet has offered . . . [internment revisionists] access to a whole new audience.*

Other conservatives, like Shonin Yamashita, a San Diego resident who was interned in the camp at Poston, Ariz., suggested a "forgive and forget" approach. "Even most of those who say 'Jap' do not mean to insult us at all," Yamashita argues. "Why can't we just laugh it off? We lose more friends by protesting."

Sadly, members of Baker's own camp didn't always heed Yamashita's pleas for civility. Baker became infamous within the Japanese American community for her disruptive behavior at commission hearings on redress and the development of the Manzanar site, where she would often become verbally abusive and need to be restrained by security personnel. Following Baker's lead, Baker supporter Howard Garber had to be forcibly removed from a 1996 commission meeting after he began yelling profanities and screaming "Where's the media! Why isn't this meeting being publicized?"

Of course, Baker herself had an explanation for the media silence: a government conspiracy that reached to the top levels of the U.S. political system. To illustrate her theory, Baker dredged up stories of how dissenting testimony about the camps was "held silent by political subterfuge," citing a memo sent by Jesse Helms to the Oval Office that was supposedly "waylaid and/or covered-up by scandalous means." (At press time, Helms' staff could not confirm whether such a memo was ever sent.) A more benign explanation for the alleged cover-up would be that most politicians and media gatekeepers just ignored Baker's voluminous mailings because of their hateful tone and weird conspiracy theories.

Web of Infamy

Although Baker depended on expensive and labor-intensive mailings to spread the revisionist word, the Internet has offered Baker's disciples access to a whole new audience for a fraction of the cost.

One of the most complete Web sites on the subject is maintained by the *Webb Research Group*, an Oregon-based publishing house that prints Baker's most popular revisionist texts and specializes in niche books about 19th-century Oregon history, *Japanese Attacks on U.S. Soil*, and other books of local interest. The Web site promos are written in the same hyperbolic language as the author's own writings, and describe Baker's work as "SO important that it resides in a special archive set aside at The Lillian Baker Collection at the Hoover Institution for War, Revolution and Peace at Stanford University."

So important? Special archive? "Oh, I hope you won't say that," laughs Carol Leadenham, assistant archivist at the Hoover Institution, patiently explaining the library's archival procedures—essentially, to collect anything with any research value on a given topic—and pointing out that Baker is a small part of Stanford's huge, incredibly diverse holdings on the Japanese American camp experience. "Her books are not in a special collection," she emphasizes. "She's one of 4,000 collections." (Similarly, the Web site's claim that "the California Legislature is so afraid of [Baker's] books that they've been banned in California public schools!" was shot down by Barbara Jeffus, school library consultant for the California Department of Education.)

New Recruits

But probably none of these small details will deter the surviving members of Baker's camp, or her posthumous new recruits. Although both Embrey and Michael report less activity from Baker's old guard of World War II veterans recently, a small group of Vietnam veterans has threatened to burn down buildings at the Manzanar site, and recently more angry letters have been coming from writers living outside of the Inyo County area.

Nor is the old guard packing it in. W.W. Hastings, a self-described "very extensive combat veteran" and heir apparent to the Lillian Baker legacy, has continued to be one of the most vocal opponents of the Manzanar historic site. A prolific letter writer, Hasting has written numerous typo-ridden letters to his local paper, the *Inyo Register*, castigating the "dedicated [Japanese] fanatics willing to starve and dye to defend Japan and the Emporer" and the museum personnel who are "acting like flower children of the 1960's lacking character and integerity."

Michael, who is very familiar with Hastings' work, doesn't put a lot of stock in the man's editorial comments—or even his grasp on reality. "In letters to the editor, he's recounted conversations he's had with John Muir," Michael says, noting that Hastings is clearly not old enough—he was born in 1922—to have had a heart-to-heart with the famed naturalist. "John Muir died in 1914," he says with a laugh. "He's not playing with a full deck."

For Further Research

Books

Paul Bailey, *City in the Sun: The Japanese Concentration Camp at Poston, Arizona.* Los Angeles: Westernlore Press, 1971.

Lillian Baker and Karl R. Bendetsen, *American and Japanese Relocation in World War II: Fact, Fiction & Fallacy.* Medford, OR: Webb Research Group, 1998.

Francis Biddle, *In Brief Authority.* Garden City, NY: Doubleday, 1962.

Gordon H. Chang, ed., *Morning Glory, Evening Shadow: Yamato Ichihashi and His Internment Writings, 1942–1945.* Stanford, CA: Stanford University Press, 1997.

Commission on Wartime Relocation and Internment of Civilians, *Personal Justice Denied.* Washington, DC: Government Printing Office, 1983.

Stetson Conn, *The Decision to Evacuate the Japanese from the Pacific Coast.* Washington, DC: Center of Military History, U.S. Army, 1990.

Roger Daniels, *Prisoners Without Trial: Japanese-Americans in World War II.* New York: Hill and Wang, 1993.

Roger Daniels, ed., *American Concentration Camps: A Documentary History of the Relocation and Incarceration of Japanese-Americans, 1942–1945.* New York: Garland, 1989.

Roger Daniels, Sandra C. Taylor, and Harry H.L. Kitano, eds., *Japanese Americans: From Relocation to Redress.* Seattle: University of Washington Press, 1991.

C. Harvey Gardiner, *Pawns in a Triangle of Hate: The Peruvian Japanese and the United States.* Seattle: University of Washington Press, 1981.

Audrey Girdner and Anne Loftis, *The Great Betrayal: The Evacuation of the Japanese-Americans During World War II.* New York: Macmillan, 1969.

Bryan J. Grapes, ed., *Japanese American Internment Camps: History Firsthand.* San Diego: Greenhaven Press, 2001.

Leslie T. Hatamiya, *Righting a Wrong: Japanese Americans and the Passage of the Civil Liberties Act of 1988.* Stanford, CA: Stanford University Press, 1993.

William Hohri, *Repairing America: An Account of the Movement for Japanese-American Redress*. Pullman, WA: Washington State University Press, 1988.

Bill Hosokawa, *JACL in Quest of Justice*. New York: William Morrow, 1982.

Jeanne Wakatsuki Houston and James D. Houston, *Farewell to Manzanar*. Boston: Houghton Mifflin, 1973.

Peter Irons, *Justice at War*. Berkeley: University of California Press, 1993.

Charles McClain, *The Mass Internment of Japanese Americans and the Quest for Legal Redress*. New York: Garland, 1994.

Alice Yang Murray, ed., *What Did the Internment of Japanese Americans Mean?* Boston: Bedford/St. Martin's, 2000.

Dillon S. Myer, *Uprooted Americans: The Japanese Americans and the War Relocation Authority During World War II*. Tucson: University of Arizona Press, 1971.

Douglas W. Nelson, *Heart Mountain: The Story of an American Concentration Camp*. Madison: State Historical Society of Wisconsin, 1976.

Richard S. Nishimoto, edited by Lane Ryo Hirabayashi, *Inside an American Concentration Camp: Japanese American Resistance at Poston, Arizona*. Tucson: University of Arizona Press, 1995.

Page Smith, *Democracy on Trial*. New York: Simon & Schuster, 1995.

Edward H. Spicer et al., *Impounded People: Japanese-Americans in Relocation Centers*. Tucson: University of Arizona Press, 1969.

John Tateishi, ed., *And Justice for All: An Oral History of the Japanese American Detention Camps*. Seattle: University of Washington Press, 1984.

Michi Weglyn, *Years of Infamy: The Untold Story of America's Concentration Camps*. Seattle: University of Washington Press, 1996.

Periodicals

Russell E. Bearden, "One State's Reaction to Wartime Internment," *Journal of the West*, April 2000.

Boston College Law Review, "Symposium: The Long Shadow of Korematsu," December 1998.

Francis X. Clines, "A Memorial Addresses a Wrong," *New York Times*, October 24, 1999.

Mark Gonzalez, "The Constitutionalism of Racism: The

Hirabayashi and Korematsu Decisions," *Race and Class*, January/March 2001.

Lon Yuki Kurashige, "America's Concentration Camps: Remembering the Japanese American Experience," *Journal of American History*, June 1996.

Cliff Lewis, "John Steinbeck's Alternative to Internment Camps: A Policy for the President, *Journal of the West*, January 1995.

Timothy P. Maga, "Ronald Reagan and the Redress for Japanese-American Internment," *Presidential Studies Quarterly*, Summer 1998.

Jamin B. Raskin, "A Precedent for Arab-Americans?" *Nation*, February 4, 1991.

Alice Dundes Rentlen, "A Psychohistorical Analysis of the Japanese American Internment," *Human Rights Quarterly*, November 1995.

Somini Sengupta, "What Is a Concentration Camp? Ellis Island Exhibit Prompts a Debate," *New York Times*, March 8, 1998.

Robert Shaffer, "Opposition to Internment: Defending Japanese American Rights During World War II," *Historian*, Spring 1999.

Eric J. Sundquist, "The Japanese-American Internment: A Reappraisal," *American Scholar*, August 1988.

Julie Tamaki, "Internment of Japanese Americans Still Hurts," *Los Angeles Times*, October 24, 1999.

Jon Wiener, "Hard Times at Heart Mountain," *Nation*, May 15, 1995.

Ronald W. Yoshino, "Barbed Wire and Beyond: A Sojourn Through Internment—A Personal Reflection," *Journal of the West*, January 1996.

Index